EMPOWER

EMPOWER

CONQUERING THE DISEASE OF FEAR

TAREQ AZIM

WITH SETH DAVIS

ATRIA BOOKS

NEW YORK • LONDON • TORONTO • SYDNEY • NEW DELHI

An Imprint of Simon & Schuster, Inc.
1230 Avenue of the Americas
New York, NY 10020

First Atria Books hardcover edition January 2022

ATRIA B O O K S and colophon are trademarks of Simon & Schuster, Inc.

For information about special discounts for bulk purchases, please
contact Simon & Schuster Special Sales at 1-866-506-1949 or
business@simonandschuster.com.

The Simon & Schuster Speakers Bureau can bring authors to your live
event. For more information, or to book an event, contact the Simon
& Schuster Speakers Bureau at 1-866-248-3049 or visit our website at
www.simonspeakers.com.

Interior design by Dana Sloan

Manufactured in the United States of America

1 3 5 7 9 10 8 6 4 2

Library of Congress Cataloging-in-Publication Data
Names: Azim, Tareq, author. | Davis, Seth, author.
Title: Empower : conquering the disease of fear / by Tareq Azim;
with Seth Davis.
Description: First Atria Books hardcover edition. | New York, NY:
Atria Books, [2022]
Identifiers: LCCN 2021030429 (print) | LCCN 2021030430 (ebook) |
ISBN 9781982150648 (hardcover) | ISBN 9781982150655
(paperback) | ISBN 9781982150679 (ebook)
Subjects: LCSH: Azim, Tareq. | Refugees—Afghanistan. |
Refugees—United States. | Afghans—United States—Biography. |
Self-esteem. | Self-realization.
Classification: LCC HV640.5.A28 A95 2022 (print) |
LCC HV640.5.A28 (ebook) | DDC 362.87809581—dc23
LC record available at https://lccn.loc.gov/2021030429
LC ebook record available at https://lccn.loc.gov/2021030430

ISBN 978-1-9821-5064-8
ISBN 978-1-9821-5067-9 (ebook)

This book is dedicated to my dear queen and grandmother,
my "Bebe," Mahbooba Sara Wali.

None of this would have been possible without the discipline,
unconditional love, and independence you have shown. You lost
your father when you were three and were widowed when you
were thirty-six, yet you carried your children on your shoulders
out of Afghanistan and through the refugee camps because you
wanted to give your family a new life in the United States.
And here we are today, all thanks to you, my queen. I love you.

Fear does not prevent death. It prevents life.

—*Buddha*

CONTENTS

FOREWORD

In the fall of 2019, I decided to come out of retirement for a second time and play the last few games of the season with the Seattle Seahawks. I was thirty-three years old and believed I still had some yards left in me, but I also had a major problem: I was *way* out of shape. I even got a little breathless walking up the steps inside the Seahawks office building. Not only that, I only had two weeks to get ready. I needed a game plan, bad, and there was only one guy who could help me put it together. So I called him immediately.

"Yo, T," I said. "Time to get to work."

I had known Tareq Azim for about nine years. He had gotten me through some tough times, and he knew better than anyone what my body was capable of doing. So we got to work, and after two weeks, when Tareq told me I was ready, I believed him. I believe every word that man says. He has earned that trust a thousand times over. He's not just a trainer to me, and he's much more than a friend. He's my brother.

I'm not the only one who feels this way about Tareq. When you stepped into his gym at Empower, you understood you were going to work with someone who was totally committed to strengthening your mind, body, and spirit. You also knew you were joining forces with a community of dreamers, which included not just professional football players and Mixed Martial Arts fighters but also powerful executives, innovative entrepreneurs, popular entertainers, and people from all walks of life who were seeking to be challenged. So many people spend their lives trying to run from their fears, or even denying they exist in the first place. For Tareq, fear isn't just a feeling, it's a disease. He teaches his teammates to run *toward* their fears, not so they can get rid of them but so they can acknowledge them, embrace them, and change the narrative around them.

Now it's your turn. By acquiring this book, you are ready to be empowered the same way. In these pages you will not only read about Tareq's philosophies and principles, you will learn the incredible story of his family, his heritage, his values, and his fight to use sports as a way to bring the world together and conquer the disease of fear. I can tell you firsthand that this book was written by an extraordinary individual. We're talking about a guy who grew up as the son of Afghan refugees in San Francisco, went to Afghanistan to help his father with some major problems, and then while he was there figured he should start a women's boxing federation in the country, which required a meeting with a Taliban warlord. Tareq knows all about fear, but he works every day to conquer the disease.

I can tell you from playing many years in the NFL that we

need a new narrative around the topic of mental health. Walk into any NFL locker room, and you will find fifty-three of the strongest dudes you will ever meet in your life. But somehow too many of us have become convinced that if you show fear, vulnerability, anxiety, depression, or any other type of mental health challenge, then that is an admission of weakness. Tareq wants to change the narrative so that acknowledging your fears isn't seen as an act of weakness but rather as the ultimate act of strength. Thinking that those feelings and fears somehow make you less strong or less manly—that's a disease, man. That's what needs to be conquered.

This is why Tareq and I connected on such a primal level from our very first game plan. I was playing for the Seahawks, and I was introduced to Tareq by Tom Cable, an offensive genius who was working as our assistant head coach, offensive line coach, and run game coordinator. Tom didn't tell Tareq that much about me or instruct him as to what he should say to me. He simply told Tareq, "You'll figure it out." Tareq was straight-up honest with me from our very first conversation. I pounded my heart, it felt so good. From that day forward, Tareq and I went to work. It's funny, because you hear about this legendary trainer and you think you're going to set up with him and use all this fancy equipment and these weird techniques. Then you walk into his gym and it's almost empty. You think you're really strong and he says, "Show me how many push-ups you can do on your fingertips." That humbles you real quick.

When you're around Tareq, you learn to be comfortable in your discomfort. You learn to feel strength when you're vulnerable. Tareq knew how important it was for me to use my football talents to serve the community where I grew up in Oakland. Most people encourage you to take what you can get, but Tareq encouraged me to be selfless. When I tried to pay him, he got angry. "You said we were family," he told me. "Don't insult me this way." To this day he won't take any money from me. The dude is the real thing. There's no halfway commitment with him. It's all the way or no way.

One of the reasons Tareq and I clicked is that we both believe in the importance of family. With him, that isn't just talk. His whole life is dedicated to serving his family. His sister worked with him at Empower, and his brother, who is a police officer, was always around. After a few weeks of working together, I went to Tareq's house and met his parents. Talk about amazing people. Tareq's father was the perfect example of quiet, gentle strength. He gave his son quite a legacy, and Tareq has spent his adult life fulfilling it.

When Tareq told me he was going to write a book, my first thought was *It's about damn time*. For a long time he just wanted to work behind the scenes and not make all of this about him. Eventually he realized that he has seen too much and learned too many important things to keep it to himself. This isn't about Tareq seizing glory, it's about him spreading his truth and empowering the world to conquer the disease of fear. That's some deep stuff right there, but it's damn important.

So I'm glad you've got this book because of the empowerment it will give to you. But I also hope that, by reading it, you will feel empowered to help others. I'm counting on you to carry this book like I carried the football—with strength, determination, speed, and, most of all, peace of mind. I hope that by reading it you'll be able to change your own narrative and then become someone who helps those you care about to find their truths as well. Let Tareq's story become your story. Let his message become your message. Let his mission become your mission.

Time to get to work.

—Marshawn Lynch

EMPOWER

SMILING AT DEATH

My father, Sayed Azim, often told me that I saved his life. He had been sinking into a deep depression, but when I was born he felt like he needed to stay alive. I understood from a very young age that he was very fragile. His gentle, loving nature led others, including close members of his family, to take advantage of him. It was up to me to be his protector.

When I was growing up my friends used to ask me, "Why are you so crazy about your dad?" It was hard to make them understand. My whole life, my number one fear was that something bad would happen to him. No matter what, I couldn't let him die. If he did, it would mean that I failed.

My father and mother both grew up in Afghanistan as the descendants of prominent citizens who contributed tremendously to one of the few recent periods of stability the country has seen. When the Soviet Union invaded in 1979, they were cast off as refugees. They moved to Germany, where I was born in 1982. Two years later we came to America. We settled in the Bay Area of California, where my parents, my older sister, Dina, and younger brother, Yossef, and I lived in Section 8 housing. We bought our groceries with food stamps. I must have lived in a dozen different houses and apartments by the time I was a senior in high school because the housing authority kept moving us around. We'd go from this beautiful three-bedroom house to a ghetto-ass two-bedroom apartment in the 'hood. And you never knew when it would happen. I would come home from school and there would be a U-Haul truck outside our house.

My parents were lucky to escape Afghanistan when they did, but my father had a lot of very serious mental problems throughout his life. He had an enormous amount of stress to deal with and spent significant time in psych wards and mental institutions. Later in life he developed progressive supranuclear palsy, a degenerative brain disease. He was also a diabetic and developed renal failure later in life. He was a highly medicated man, to say the least.

And yet, to me he seemed larger-than-life, a man of superhuman strength and fortitude. We were extremely close. He shared in every failure and every ounce of success I ever had. He was so proud to see me become one of the few Afghan American Division I football players, attend Fresno State, and start my own business developing and promoting competitive fighters, NFL players, and scores of high-powered business executives. But eventually his health issues caught up to him. In 2012, when he was sixty-one years old, his body went into a slow and steady decline. I could see him slipping away. My worst nightmare was coming true, and there was nothing I could do about it.

My siblings, my mom, and I tried as hard as we could to keep him alive. My entire existence was dedicated to training the human mind to conquer any obstacle. Why couldn't I save my father from death? Everything I had accomplished in life, I had done through the sheer force of my will. I remember one point in late 2013 when my dad was in the hospital yet again, and he had to go on life support, but he came through like a champ and we took him home. On another occasion, his doctor came in the room and told me he wanted to make my dad "comfortable." I wasn't clear on what he was saying, so he explained to me they were basically going to impose a slow, sleepy death on him. That was the wrong thing to say. I got up in his face, called him a punk-ass this and that, and berated him for making the suggestion. My dad was lying in his bed and said gently, "That's okay, don't let this bother you." We moved my dad to an assisted-living facility where they focused more on his physical and functional health. Comfortable, my ass.

My dad fought as hard as he could, but it got to the point where I realized he wasn't doing it because he wanted to stay alive. He was fighting for me, my siblings, and my mother. He had been on kidney dialysis for about six years. On January 7, 2014, I got a call from the dialysis center saying I should come there right away to deal with an urgent situation. I sped out there and pulled into the driveway. My uncle Ehsan, my mother's brother, was holding my father's hand. My father was saying to my uncle in Pashto, our native tongue, "My dear brother, I've had it. It's enough."

That was a punch in the gut. I realized it was selfish of me to try so hard to keep my dad alive. He was miserable. It got to a point where they were having a hard time finding veins in his arms to give him the dialysis. His spirit dropped big-time. All he wanted was our blessings to go. My uncle tried to explain this to me, but he had a hard time getting the words out. He knew how I felt about my father.

We had a family meeting with the doctors. They told us that my father didn't want the dialysis anymore and that if he didn't get it, his body would start shutting down. My mom, my two siblings, my uncle, and a few cousins were all in this room looking at me to make the decision. My father had given me, his protector, sole power of attorney over his affairs. That meant it was totally my call. Was I really supposed to pull the plug on my own father? My hero? Was that what my family was telling me to do?

I didn't want them to see me cry, so I bolted out of the hospital, got inside my car, and bawled. I was screaming. Snot and spit was flying. I had suffered some disappointments in my life, but to that point I had never experienced real heartbreak. I've tried to explain this to my friends. How would you feel if one of your kids died? That's how I feared I would feel when my father's turn came.

In the end, as painful as it was, I granted my father's wish. I signed off on the decision to cease his dialysis treatments. We brought him home so he could die in peace.

His body shut down very fast, just as the doctor said it would. A hospice nurse came to the house to keep him comfortable. We set him up in the living room of the house so friends and family could visit him. After a couple of days, he asked Yossef to take him up to his bedroom and lie with him. "Tell Tareq to be strong," he said. "And to start planning my funeral. It's time for me to go."

We carried him up the stairs and into his bedroom. He called me, my mom, my sister, and my brother to his bed. We had the most epic conversation a family could have. It was so beautiful. We were sitting in his room, joking, laughing, talking shit, making fun of each other. He looked at my mom and said, "If I had any shortcomings as a husband and your partner and the father of your children, I want to apologize and ask for your forgiveness." My mom said the same thing back to him. It was the first time I heard them say "I love you" to each other.

At around ten o'clock something incredible happened. My dad got out of bed and tried to walk to the bathroom. I spoke about it with Carol Cable, whose husband, Tom, was an assistant coach with the Seattle Seahawks at the time. Carol is like a second mother to me. She used to run a hospice business so she knew all about this process. Carol told me that my father appeared to be having what is sometimes called a "last hurrah." That's a burst of euphoria but the patient knows the end is coming.

The next day, I left the house to train one of my fighters. We went across the street to a park to get a workout in. We were doing some pad work when my brother started calling me frantically. He told me to rush home.

When I reached my father's bedroom, my maternal grandmother was rubbing his head and praying. She was reciting the Surah Yasin Sharif prayer, which is said at Muslim funerals. My dad was taking some hard breaths, fighting for his life. For the next several hours, I didn't move from his bedside. The room was packed with cousins and relatives and friends.

At around midnight, everyone left, so it was just me, my mom, my brother, and my sister. As the time passed, he continued to struggle to breathe. I was holding him and kissing him. Finally the nurse said to me, "Tareq, do you love Baba?"

"Of course."

"He's fighting for you, sweetheart. You need to give him permission to let go."

I hugged him close again, kissed him, and said, "Go to your mom and your dad. We're going to be fine."

A few minutes later, he let out a long breath and dropped his head to his left. As he went to the next world, I stared right into my father's face.

He was smiling.

I turned to my family and said, "I think he just went to heaven."

My brother said, "No, no, look. He's smiling."

"No, man," I replied. "I think he just took his last breath."

My mom put a mirror under his nose, and sure enough, he was gone.

We looked at each other and sort of giggled. Like, what just happened? Look at him! He died with a smile on his face. It's still there!

It was surreal. The nurse came up and wrote down the time. I took a strip of fabric and wrapped it around my father's head to keep his jaw closed. That made his smile turn up even more. I helped tie him up while my family called my uncles and cousins and other family members. They all rushed back to the house and saw the smiling dead man for themselves.

Later on in the evening, the room was empty again. I sat next to my father and had a conversation that felt like he was still with me. "Dad, I don't want your spirit to leave sad," I said. "I don't want your spirit to leave angry. I just want you to know that I believe your whole existence was about this moment right here. It was this moment that you taught me the lesson that the whole purpose of life is to be able to die content."

My whole life I swore I would blow my brains out if I ever let my father die. I was so worried he would be frightened and there would be nothing I could do about it. It was my sacred duty to be strong for him. In the end, he was a million times stronger than I ever imagined. He left on his own terms, and that made things safe for us.

All this time, I was trying to save him. By smiling at death, he ended up saving me.

Fear is the biggest driving force in our lives. To be fearful is to be human. It is literally the first feeling we have when we are born. We are ripped from the warmth of our mothers' wombs and brought into the scary, bright, cold world, where we have to breathe and eat on our own for the first time. Yet, so much of our life is devoted to getting rid of fear. This is the exact opposite of what we should do. Instead of fighting fear, we should embrace it.

If we let fear dictate how we act and think, it becomes a disease. By embracing fear, we conquer the disease of fear. There is no other way.

What is it that we fear the most? The answer is easy: death. An abiding fear of death is the source of a great many problems for people. It leads to depression and anxiety, as well as bad decisions. And yet, death is inescapable. We are all going to die. There is only one thing we get to take to our graves, and that is a feeling. How do we want to feel when we die? Do we want to be afraid? Or do we want to die smiling?

Seeing my father smile at death was an enormous revelation for me. It gave me a brand-new purpose. That has led me to places that my father could never have imagined for me. I have built a successful business, but more than that, I have created a new paradigm for thinking, training, competing, and feeling. I work with professional athletes, prominent businessmen, powerful politicians, famous entertainers, and every type of person in between—rich and poor, accomplished and addicted, famous and anonymous, tall and short, strong and weak, fast and slow. For all of those differences, the traits I notice most are the ones that bind us together. I see our common humanity.

Don't misunderstand me. I am not saying we should be fixated on death. That can be dark and depressing, and ultimately defeating. What I am inviting you to do is to face your fear of death, which is the root of all of our fears. We cannot escape fear any more than we can escape death. If my father can smile at death, then you can smile at your fears. You can conquer this disease.

When I start working with a new client—I prefer to call them teammates—one of the first things I say to them is "Let's do a game plan." This is an invitation to share our personal experiences, talk about our fears, and then set goals and plot a path forward. These are basically just honest conversations, but I call them game plans because I don't want to scare people off. Who wants to have honest conversations—I mean *really* honest conversations? You know that expression "The truth hurts"? That's how people instinctively feel, which is unfortunate. The only way to find our purpose and fulfill our potential is by living our truths. A game plan is the road map to that life. It is the first step toward conquering the disease of fear.

What, you might ask, does all this have to do with preparing people for fights and NFL games? The answer is that physical activity brings you to the depths of understanding character and human ability. I teach my teammates to push through discomfort, because this is what we have to do in life. When someone comes to me, they know they're going to hurt and bleed and sweat, but they will know there is a game plan behind that.

For all of my adult life, I have devoted myself to developing game plans with family, friends, clients, partners, and teammates. I have traveled the world spreading my message and learning from experiences. That includes four and a half years spent in Afghanistan, where I used sports to bind up the wounds of a war-ravaged society. I even established an Afghan women's boxing federation to prove that sports could drive meaningful social change. I didn't quite create world peace, but I did touch a lot of hearts, and in turn I achieved clarity about what my life's work should be.

For a long time, I did all this work in private. I trained world-class fighters, NFL all-pros, and other celebrities, but tried to keep a low profile. Journalists would reach out and want to tell my story, but I always declined. My father taught me to be humble as well as strong. But over time I realized that this message was too important to keep to myself. That's why I wrote this book. There are too many people in this world dying from sadness. It really and truly doesn't have to be this way.

My purpose with this book is to share my story so that you,

the reader, will feel understood. I want you to be at peace knowing that we all have struggles. We all have sickness. We all have worries. We all have fear. It's easy to feel like we are not in control—because we're not. When you are done reading, I hope you will experience the freedom of feeling however you want to feel. I hope you will decide that when your time comes you will smile at death. I hope you will conquer the disease of fear.

Let's do a game plan.

CHAPTER ONE

TRUTH

I was in the second grade when I first came face-to-face with the truth.

It happened the night we visited my mom at her job as a hostess at a local Indian restaurant. She was always working two or three jobs to help support the family, yet she still did all the cooking and housework that mothers so often do. On this particular evening, she wasn't able to cook dinner for us, so she told us to meet her at the restaurant. My sister, my brother, and my father all went there and sat at a table together.

The restaurant was next to a bowling alley in our hometown of Concord, California. It was a dark, classy little place with red candles all around. When the restaurant's owner saw us, he was not pleased. He went over to my mom and told her we had to leave. I guess he wanted this to be a nice, upscale joint, and that image in his mind did not include a table full of refugees from Afghanistan.

I felt bad for my mom when I heard what he said. I was young, but I didn't want things to be awkward for her. Neither did my dad, so he told us to get up and leave. He was the least confrontational person I have ever known, but my mom wasn't having it. She quit her job right on the spot, threw off her apron, and took me, my brother, and my sister by the hands.

My mom would never tolerate us being insulted like that. Her feeling was *If my boss does not want my family around, then this is not a place where I want to work.* I remember my dad had this smirk on his face as we walked out. He was so proud of my her for not letting the need for a paycheck take away her honor. We ended up eating at a McDonald's across the street.

My dad, Sayed, on the other hand, was a gentle soul, just the sweetest human being in the world. From a very young age, I thought of myself as his protector because he was so easy to take advantage of. He had no idea how powerful he was, how handsome he was, how smart he was. He was very quiet and kept a lot of things to himself. I used to think of this as weakness, but now I understand the roots of his behavior. I had no idea at the time that he had come from a family in Afghanistan that was considered nobility, that he owned enormous areas of land that should have made him wealthy. It wasn't until my late teens that he finally told me how his family had walked all over him and tried to take his land for themselves. He depended on me to give him strength.

My mom was the daughter of a prominent Afghan general named Shah Wali. He was the first commanding jet fighter pilot in the history of Afghanistan and played an instrumental part in developing Bagram Air Base. The general was very respected and revered, which made him a prime target when the Soviets invaded and took over the country in 1979.

There's a reason I didn't know how much land and money my father had until I was much older. He never wanted us to feel entitled to that wealth or show a bad work ethic because we felt like we had something coming down the road. I can never thank him enough for that. Because of him, I work as hard as anybody I know and surround myself with people who push the concept of work ethic to a level I didn't know existed.

My parents were disruptors before I had any concept of what that meant. On the one hand, they made sure we honored our Afghan heritage and spoke our native languages in the home. On the other hand, they made us do all the things American kids were doing. My parents didn't want us thinking that the American kids were any better than us. We joined martial arts programs, played in soccer clubs, went camping, and got involved in lots of school activities. That was an unusual approach in our Afghan community. The other kids thought of them as the "cool" parents. So did my brother, my sister, and me.

That is, until it came to the really fun stuff. My parents were so strict, I never got to spend the night at a friend's house until I was a junior in high school. They wanted to make sure we didn't get into drinking and smoking dope like a lot of the kids were. I was always angry about that, but Mom explained that it was very important to protect our family name, that we could never do anything to disrespect our grandfather's spirit.

When she said that, it made me realize that not only were we different because we were part of an Afghan community in America but even *inside* that community we were different as well. Talk about an overpowering truth.

This is why I've never wanted to play victim. I saw a lot of my friends and cousins adopt that mentality, and it led them to do stupid shit like join gangs and break car windows, like they were out to get revenge on all those people who did them wrong. I despised that culture of entitlement. These were young people who were lucky enough to grow up in America. They couldn't even comprehend living anywhere else. Meanwhile, their parents hadn't had those same opportunities and were busting their asses to provide for their children. The difference in my family was that my parents were really engaged with us. They wanted to know what we were doing. They saw every report card. I didn't like when they were strict sometimes, but I still never wanted to let them down. That would have been an insult to my family heritage.

It's easy to say now how much these things helped me, but imagine learning these truths beginning at the age of seven. Whenever I acted up, I got my ass whupped. It sucked, but they always told me *why* they were doing these things. I knew my parents loved me, but I always felt like I had to earn their love. So when I got it, that made it much sweeter.

So I don't like when I see people complain about how bad they have it. Yeah, shit happens, and life isn't fair for a lot of minorities, immigrants, refugees, or people like me who grew up in tough circumstances. In my case, when someone did me wrong, that just added fuel to my fire. I was determined that there would come a time when I was dependent on no one. If anything, people were going to be dependent on me. They would be eating out of my hand. Someday that would be my truth.

————

One day when I was nine years old, my cousin Sal and I were riding our bikes. As we came down a hill, I spotted a massive fig tree. My dad always loved figs, so I told Sal to stop so I could grab a bunch to take home to him. I took so many that I had to curl up my shirt to hold them all. I rode the bike with the shirt in my mouth. I couldn't wait to show those figs to my papa.

I ran inside the house so excited, but when I shouted up to my dad that I had gotten him figs, he didn't answer. I went upstairs to his bedroom and he was sitting Indian-style, staring at the wall. I called out to him, but he didn't reply. I reached up and touched his face, but that only made him more tense. He clenched his jaw and balled up his fists. Sal was standing there with me, and he was as shocked as I was. He wrapped his arm around my shoulder and neck. When I called out to my father again, he didn't respond. When I touched him, he felt like a brick wall. It was frightening.

I called 9-1-1 and told the operator, "I don't know what to do. My dad is awake and he isn't talking." They sent over an ambulance. I called my relatives crying, and a few of them came over. When the ambulance got there, the paramedics sent me downstairs. I was standing outside with my cousin. Next thing I knew, they were taking my dad out of the house in a straitjacket. As soon as I saw that, I started bawling. This was my dad! My hero! I thought they were going to take him somewhere and that he would be gone forever.

At that point, my dad must have snapped out of whatever was happening because he started arguing on his behalf that he wasn't sick and he wanted to stay. It wasn't easy because his English was very rough. Looking back, I think he was having an intense anxiety attack. Whatever was going on, it wasn't normal.

Back then, treatment for mental illness was pretty harsh and primitive. There was so much shame attached to it. The paramedics took him to a mental hospital in Richmond, California. The next day, my mom took us to visit him.

As you can imagine, it was a very traumatic experience. There were a lot of very sick people in that place. I thought they were a bunch of weirdos, and I couldn't bear seeing my dad in there. They were walking up to him and looking at him real strangely and petting him. My dad was such a good soul. He kept telling us, "Don't worry, they're good people, don't be scared." But I could see he felt embarrassed and helpless.

From that day on, I determined that my father would never feel that way again, ever. Not if I could help it.

That's the thing about mental illness. It can be a huge burden on a family. My mother had a lot of mental struggles, too, so my brother, my sister, and I had to grow up real fast. It's hard to know for sure what the onset was for my parents' illnesses, but I'm sure it stemmed from the trauma of going from royalty to peasants in twenty-four hours with no warning or preparation. Until that point, my mom had a cook her whole life. She didn't know anything about preparing food for her children. She would always be scarred by the memory of the night a group of soldiers barged into her house looking for her father, the famous general. They were

Afghans who were working for the communists. You'd think my mom would have cowered in fear, but instead she was talking all kinds of shit, calling them corrupt sellouts. One of them stuck an AK-47 in her mouth to shut her up.

What they didn't know was that the general was in the back of the house. When he stepped out, the guys practically shit themselves. My grandfather went up to each one of them and slapped him. The guys never even made eye contact, they were so ashamed. But they did their job and took my grandfather out of the house. My mother never saw him again.

My mom's issues weren't quite as bad as my dad's, but they stemmed from heartbreak. She had a lot of anxiety and flashbacks. She is still alive, and this has continued to be a lifelong battle.

This was a big part of my truth, not only during my childhood but well into adulthood. It taught me the importance of seeing clearly who I am, where I came from, and the battles I must fight. One truth I have really come to know is that mental illness is real. It comes in many forms, and it fuels all sorts of destructive behavior. That includes addictions. When someone is addicted to something, it overtakes their entire lives. Nothing is more important than feeding that addiction—not work, not family, not relationships, not money, not health. So in order to help them overcome their addictions, I must first try to get them to face their own hard-core truths.

———

When I start my first game plan with a new teammate, my first objective is to get him or her to understand that there is no need to be frightened of the truth. Truth is liberating. Truth is empowering. There is no healing without it.

Is it painful to face the truth? Of course. Just like it's painful to do a squat with five hundred pounds of steel on your back. How do you feel after you do a hundred push-ups? Hurts, doesn't it? You've torn your muscle fibers apart, stretched your tendons and ligaments, built up a ton of lactic acid, gotten your heart rate way up. But what's the result of all that? You've got some big thighs and chest muscles that come in real handy when you're trying to knock a running back on his ass.

When I tell you that you need to find your truth, you're probably intimidated, right? Truth is the last thing you want to find. We are taught that the truth hurts. I say the truth *should* hurt. This is why I believe we need to recondition our language. If we say the truth is going to hurt, then people will avoid it.

It's like when you played the game Truth or Dare. I always took the dare, and I'll bet you did, too. No one wants to be asked if they like a girl or a guy. No one wants to be made fun of in front of their friends. Truth is scary because we have a fear of being judged and of having something exposed that can be used against us.

And yet, we must learn the truth because that's what defines our purpose. Why do I want to laugh? Why do I want to grow? Why do I want to be happy? Why do I want to be loved? I want to teach people that truth is not something they should not fear. It's something they should embrace.

Most people would describe me as a trainer, but I find that label to be very limiting. I like to consider myself whatever people want to consider me. I coach and I instruct, but I don't want hobbyists. You're not going to come to me just to burn off a couple of calories. If the teammate is from out of town, he has to fly in and spend four or five days and really commit to the process. My game plans are typically not organized in advance. I want to have natural conversations with people when I dig in.

As with everything else in my work, I bring my own personal search for truth over the course of my life. That process has also been painful at times, but it is what gave me the purpose to launch my business and dedicate myself to broadcasting my message of hope and health around the world.

I was immersed in this kind of work when, in the summer of 2015, I joined forces with a teammate whose enormous gifts were coexisting in his soul with huge demons from his past. In order to slay those demons, I had to help him face his truth.

The Game Plan: Dion Jordan Discovers His Truth

I work with a lot of NFL players, but never more than seven or so at a time. I believe that every single individual has special needs, and if he is not getting that type of attention from me, then he is wasting his money. Plus, I like to work with particular types of people—guys with "baggage." I want guys who are physical freaks but whose hearts and heads don't match up to their bodies. I want this because I know how much baggage I carry. If I can help create normalcy in their lives, it is therapeutic for me as well.

One day during the summer of 2015, I was sitting in my office at Empower, my central facility in downtown San Francisco, when an NFL agent named Doug Hendrickson showed up at the door.

Doug represents a lot of NFL players and he had been representing me for about seven years. He showed up unannounced and had one of his other clients with him. "I want you to meet Dion," he said. Turning to his client, he said, "Dion, this is Tareq." And he left.

The guy's name was Dion Jordan. I knew exactly who he was, of course. He was an All-American defensive end at the University of Oregon who was selected third in the 2013 NFL Draft by the Miami Dolphins. When he came out of college, Dion was an absolute physical specimen, standing a chiseled six-foot-six, 252 pounds, full of explosive speed and agility. The guy standing in my office that day bore very little resemblance to the Dion I thought I knew. He was run-down, disheveled, glassy-eyed, and wasting away. It made me heartbroken to see someone who was once so talented and magnificent now looking that way.

Just a few months before, Dion had been hit with a one-year suspension by the NFL for violating the league's performance-enhancing-substance policy. He had already served a four-game suspension the previous year for failing a drug test. Cut off from football, Dion had nothing but time on his hands, and it was disastrous for him. He returned to his home in Arizona and drowned himself in alcohol. He was also heavily into drugs, especially Ecstasy. Forget about playing football again. At the rate he was going, Dion was not going to be alive much longer.

As Dion was sinking further into his addictions, Doug asked Dion's girlfriend to bring Dion to San Francisco under the pretense that they were going to see a Giants baseball game. The Giants are Dion's favorite team, but the morning after the game,

Dion went into Doug's office and broke down sobbing. That was when Doug decided to bring Dion to see me at Empower, which was down the street from Doug's office at the time. He didn't even let me know he was coming.

After Doug made the introductions and left, Dion slumped into a chair. I had been through this drill many times before. There was no time for bullshit. "Do you know what it is I do here?" I asked him.

"No," he said. "I don't even know why I'm here."

I sized him up from behind my desk. I've got a nice big, comfortable office at Empower, perfect for these types of conversations. My desk is custom-made with cement, and it weighs 756 pounds. Dion was wearing a hoodie and a Giants hat. His eyes were glassy. I explained to him what I did and why. I told him about how I grew up. "I believe you are here because you want to stop feeling guilty about something," I said. "Am I right?"

Boom, the waterworks started. It poured out of his eyes like a faucet had been turned on. Dion wasn't crying or sobbing, he just let the tears flow. This was a man in deep emotional pain who immediately believed he was talking to someone who understood him on that level.

How did I know what he was feeling? Because everybody who comes to my office in that type of condition is consumed with guilt. This is the first truth they must realize. The problem is they usually don't have a safe space where they can acknowledge and address that pain, and therefore do something about it and start feeling better.

When I acknowledged to Dion that I could feel his guilt, and when he acknowledged it in return by allowing himself to be vulnerable, that was our moment of truth. That's the *power* of truth.

That first exchange lowered the waterline for us. It allowed me to dig deeper and develop his game plan. I peppered him with questions. "Why do you feel guilty? You're living with a lot of shame, right? You're embarrassed? Who have you embarrassed?" Each time he nodded and agreed, and with every prodding he opened up a little more. We were on our way.

I got up from behind my desk and gave him a big hug. I explained that we were going to get him healed but that there would be some relapses along the way and I understood that. I told him he didn't have to be scared. I think that brought him some relief knowing my expectations of him were not going to be unreasonably high. He didn't have to worry about disappointing me. We wanted to avoid setbacks wherever we could, but we didn't have to be fearful of them. We were going to conquer that disease.

It was a good meeting, but I've had good meetings before that didn't lead to any real action. I could tell Dion had a good heart, but he left my office and then I didn't hear from him for two days. I figured this was just another situation where everyone wants to help someone but no one wants to tell him the truth.

———

I understood where Dion was coming from because I had come from much the same place. He grew up in a tough area of the Hunters Point neighborhood in San Francisco. His dad was absent and his mom was a drug addict. When Dion was twelve, he and his two siblings were sent to live with an aunt in Arizona. His mom got clean and soon joined them, but it took Dion a long time to forgive her for what she had done to her family. He felt she had chosen drugs over her kids. That was a difficult truth to live with.

As if that weren't bad enough, Dion suffered severe burns over nearly half his body in 2007. He was trying to use a vacuum cleaner to siphon some gas from one car to another. The vacuum cleaner burst into flames, and soon Dion did, too. He spent a month in a burn unit in a hospital and underwent a series of skin grafts. His doctor told him he might never walk again.

So even though it was amazing that Dion later became the third pick in the 2013 NFL Draft, he still had buried a lot of hardcore truths that were generating fear—fear that he was trying to cure with alcohol and drugs. It was bad luck that he originally got drafted by the Miami Dolphins. There was no way he was going to be able to handle that South Beach scene. He was a natural-born alcoholic, but once he had all that money, he was free to try all kinds of drugs, too.

Dion first tested positive for banned substances in 2014 and was suspended for four games. The Dolphins did what they could to help him, but his addictions were too powerful. His yearlong suspension the following year cost him nearly $6 million. Unfortunately, NFL rules dictated that a player who was suspended was banned from his team's training facilities, which was the last thing Dion needed. His tendency is to completely isolate himself when things go wrong. With his support gone, he continued his lonely downward spiral.

It was during that frightening binge that Doug brought Dion into my office. Two days later, Dion showed up at Empower again.

No call, no heads-up, no nothing. Just walked in at nine thirty in the morning with a backpack over his shoulder and said, "Wassup."

This is not a man of many words. "You ready to get to work?" I asked. He nodded. I told him I had thought maybe he wasn't coming back, and he told me he was gone because he had been drinking a lot and wanted to clean up. "Perfect," I said. "Let's shake it out."

I told Dion I wanted to do some basic workouts with him for a few days, and we would progress toward developing a game plan. We started with some light body-weight activities. It didn't take long for him to break down, physically and emotionally. You have to appreciate how hard it is for a proud, competitive man who was such an Adonis to acknowledge the truth that he is so weak, and all because of bad choices that he made. I mean, this guy was a can't-miss linebacker and defensive end, and now he couldn't hold himself in a push-up position for more than a few seconds. He couldn't hold a squat without shaking. It was my job to try to help him find that buried confidence while also getting an assessment of where his body was. I understood why he was so frustrated, but I encouraged him to stay patient.

Our initial workouts lasted twenty minutes, tops, but he spent entire days with me at Empower. Much of the time was spent reading together. I got him involved in some community service projects in the Tenderloin section of the city. My brother, Yossef, is a police sergeant in that area, and he helps me connect a lot of my clients in this way. Dion also attended Alcoholics Anonymous meetings every day. I also let him come to some of our business development meetings so he could hear about investment ideas and other money management techniques. I wanted him to be

thinking about the future again and about the notion that someday he was going to be making a lot of money playing football and
needed to learn how to handle it better the second time around.

All of this was part of my plan to buy time with Dion so we
could develop our relationship. We did a lot of talking and training and reading and eating together. I've done a lot of these game
plans, but the ones I did with Dion were some of the most emotional I've ever been a part of. We sat in my office and I asked him
a lot of deep questions. I asked him what his goals were. He said
he wanted to be ripped again, to be able to explode out of a stance.
We broke down a complete training schedule that I promised
would get his body back in NFL shape—eventually.

Then I asked which mental deficiencies he wanted to strengthen
as well. "What do you mean?" he asked.

"Well," I said, "let's start with your insecurities. Do you have
anyway?"

Dion looked down at his scars from those terrible burns he
had suffered during his senior year of high school. Understanding
this experience was the key to understanding Dion—and his key
to understanding himself. Here's this huge football player and everybody thinks he can just run through walls. Inside, however,
he's broken. Those burns made it difficult for him to go shirtless
and show off his body. It gave him major confidence issues. That's
why it was so hard for him to look people in the eye. He has lived
through so many tough situations.

We delved into his emotional makeup. We talked about his
upbringing. His desire to make sure his mother never relapsed
really drove Dion, but it also overwhelmed him. When he messed

up, he knew it was inflicting pain on his mother. She was never mad at him, but she was constantly worried. That made everything worse for him.

At the end of every game plan, I ask my teammate, "What do you want me to hold you accountable for this year?" That allows me to package everything we talked about. I know at many points I am going to need triggers to keep him on the right path. "When you feel like quitting, what can I say that will make you want to keep going?"

Dion thought for a few seconds and said, "I want to make my mom smile again." And then he started bawling.

———

Only four days had passed before Dion had his first hiccup. He missed his morning appointment and I didn't hear from him for two days. He came back into my office very apologetic, and we started over again. He understood that Empower was a place of total accountability but zero judgment.

Dion moved to San Francisco and lived in the guesthouse of a friend of Doug's. He went to AA meetings every day, sometimes multiple times in a day. He met with a therapist who helped him understand that his battles with addiction were related to the fears he had developed during a difficult childhood. That was a truth that Dion needed to accept and deal with.

Our days together were long and full. He'd come to Empower in the morning, work out, and attend some of our sessions. I would take him to an Alcoholics Anonymous meeting and then back to the gym for another workout. My assignment for him was that we had to do one good deed a day. One afternoon we went to Subway, bought a hundred sandwiches, and drove all over San Francisco giving them to homeless people. We read a chapter of a book together each day. All along, I talked to Dion about his return to the NFL, not as a possibility but as a foregone conclusion. Everyone was already calling him one of the biggest busts in NFL history, but I told Dion that we would get him back there; it was just a matter of when. I wanted him to visualize it, speak it, and believe it.

We kept at it for a full year. After serving his initial suspension, Dion returned to the Dolphins for the 2016 season but he was battling an injured knee and missed the first half of the season. We were a continent apart, but we FaceTimed multiple times a day. Physically he looked great, but his confidence was still extremely delicate. He wasn't sure exactly what he was capable of, and the team was concerned as well.

He would develop these minor pains and tell his coaches he had to sit out practice. They would call me and give their reports. One day on FaceTime I told him, "Dude, this is all in your head. Your knee is fine." It took him a while to be able to trust not only the team's trainers but also his own body. Sometimes the coaches would express frustration to me when Dion got stubborn. I told them that just the fact that he was standing up for himself was a great sign.

The hiccups kept coming, as I expected. A coach from Miami called me to say Dion didn't show up to practice. This was not something I needed to wait on. My feeling is, with someone like Dion, if you don't show up for practice one day, you're probably not coming back.

Two days later, Dion called me. "My bad, bro," he said. "I'm coming to see you." He had already come back to San Francisco. We spoke briefly in my office and agreed he would come in the next day so we could get to work. At first he didn't show when we were supposed to get together, which made me wonder if something had gone wrong again. An hour later he sent me a text message that he was indeed at Empower, but I didn't know where. Turns out he was getting a massage.

I went down to the front desk and waited for him to finish his massage. He came out, and I could tell from one look at him that he had been drinking. He was acting all giddy and stupid and tried to make a joke about what I was wearing. I just shook my head and went back up to my office.

Later that night, I was at home when Dion sent me another text asking if I would see him. I told him to meet me at my office, but he refused. "I can't go in there like this," he said. I went outside and we went to my apartment down the street. I took him out to the terrace and he started crying again. He had fallen off the wagon, and his effort at getting a massage before he saw me was done in hopes of getting the smell off of him. It didn't work.

He was devastated. "I embarrassed you," he said. "This ain't okay."

He was waiting for me to tear into him, but I didn't. Instead I said, "Do you know how proud I am of you right now?" He gave me a confused look. "Look how beautiful this is," I said. "You finally acknowledged something that is valuable to you. You see value with me and you see value with Empower. You're getting emotional because all of this means something to you. You didn't have that before."

Yes, I said to him, it's not good that we had this hiccup, but we knew it was coming at some point. The fact that he realized he messed up was a massive step in his growth. For the first time in a long time, he believed his body and his life had value. So if he did something to jeopardize that, it was up to him to clean it up— but only he could do that.

Dion's confession meant the world to me. He was willing to share his truth, which meant he trusted me. I believe for the first time in his life he believed he could be vulnerable *and* safe.

Seeing Dion revert to his old, destructive behavior was painful. I was glad he found his way back, but I knew we had to make some changes. So I called Tom Cable, who at the time was an assistant head coach with the Seahawks. He is a very close friend and mentor of mine. Tom's son, Alex, had battled his own addictions and was doing very well. Tom encouraged me to keep working with Dion and try to get him back on the straight and narrow.

The Dolphins gave Dion permission to come back to San Francisco that December. Once again, we drew up a game plan and went to work. Alex Cable came down and lived with Dion for a while, which was awesome. It was just the two of them in Dion's small apartment. Alex slept on a couch and stayed with Dion all day, even going to AA meetings with him. It helped Dion stay away from alcohol, but it did not save his football career. The Dolphins released him in March.

It was because of Tom that the Seahawks decided to take a chance on Dion by signing him in April 2017. After recovering from his knee injury, which required two surgeries and extensive rehabilitation, Dion finally made his return to the NFL in December.

Ironically, it was in a road game against the Arizona Cardinals, not far from where he had lived with his family. Dion and I always had had a vision that he would get a huge sack in his very first game back, and sure enough that's exactly what happened. Dion was a man possessed that night. Considering he had been out of football for so long, it was an incredible performance. Afterward, he Face-Timed me from the team bus and said through tears, "We did it, T."

Unfortunately, that success was followed by yet another setback. In May 2019, the NFL suspended Dion for ten games for testing positive for Adderall. It was more of a clerical failure than an effort to cheat. Dion was diagnosed with ADHD when he was young, so he has taken Adderall for most of his life. That is on the NFL's banned substance list unless the player has the proper medical documentation. Dion let his documentation lapse, so once he tested positive, he was found to be in violation, which, combined with his past positive tests, led to the heavy penalty.

Dion was crushed but hardly defeated. He is in a much better, stronger place now. As I write this, he is training hard to stay in shape while he serves his suspension during the 2019 season. He is working on turning this difficult setback into a productive life lesson. His body is sculpted, down to about eight percent body fat. He got complacent with how he was feeling about himself and figured he could just take his meds and not have to take care of his business. From an alcohol standpoint, though, he has been clean. He's addicted to health now. He's not perfect, but he's evolving, and the best part is that he's no longer suffering from the disease of fear. Truth has set him free.

CHAPTER TWO

HUMILITY

There is no more helpless feeling than watching your parents suffer.

That day that I brought home all those figs to my father, only to discover him catatonic in his bedroom, revealed the depths of his mental illness. I was just a young boy, but that day I became his protector. It was a heavy-duty responsibility, but I assigned it to myself because I felt I had no other choice. It forced me to grow up faster than a lot of my friends. It also showed in stark clarity exactly where my limits were.

In other words, it taught me humility.

My father was constantly medicated. He would get better for a while, come off his meds, and then have another episode that put him right back in the psych ward. My mom would take us to visit him in the hospital, and we would spend hours with him. This went on for several years. It was gut-wrenching.

By the time I reached eighth grade, he pretty much stopped

having to be hospitalized. Things turned sour again, however, in 1999, during my senior year of high school, when he returned to Afghanistan and discovered that many of the assets he had inherited were no longer in his name. My dad spent nearly a full year trying to figure out what happened to all of his landholdings. The worst part was when he discovered that members of his family, including his own siblings, had basically robbed him. He came home and was bogged down in piecing everything together. He couldn't believe how badly he had been betrayed. Meanwhile, his kids were getting older and more independent, so he was spending more time alone than before.

That long stay in Afghanistan triggered some bad stuff for him. He had been doing so much better, but when he came back to America he started having his panic episodes again. The betrayal from family members was the worst part. These were basically a bunch of trust fund kids who had never worked a day in their lives. I can't tell you how glad I am that my parents didn't raise us like that. They made sure my sister, my brother, and I had a true work ethic.

My mom didn't have the same chemical issues my father did, but she had lived through the extreme trauma of the Soviet invasion. She was treated very badly by my father's siblings and extended family. My father was the keyholder to his family's inheritance, and his relatives saw my mom as a threat. Which was silly, because my mom had zero interest in all of that. It's why my dad was so crazy about her, because he knew she didn't have an agenda. He couldn't say that about most people.

I remember when I was in the third grade, she and my dad were having this massive argument. I walked into their room and she was sitting on the bed, just crying her eyes out. She was screaming at my dad and crying and wailing, and all of a sudden her hands crumpled up and her face twitched. She was having a stroke. I held on to her and screamed for my older sister. Then I called my uncle Tony, who came over from his house, wrapped his older sister in his arms, carried her like a baby into his car, and drove her to the emergency room.

After the stroke, my mom went into psychiatric treatment. War trauma is real, man. I saw her out of the blue reliving moments where she saw people's brains getting blown out all over again. She dealt with these emotional challenges all her adult life, and yet if you weren't in our house, you would never know it. My mom was tough. She had to be the protector, the breadwinner, the disciplinarian—everything.

My sister got it the worst of all the kids. She was the firstborn, and my mom didn't have the slightest idea how to raise a child. This was a woman who had always had everything done for her. She didn't know how to cook or drive until my sister was born. My mom was only eighteen when she had her daughter. In that first year after Dina was born, my mom became an Afghan refugee. No wonder her brain couldn't take it.

To say all of this put a strain on their marriage is a huge understatement. And yet, through all of it, my mom was a true warrior. She not only helped us through our own challenges as a family but became the de facto social worker for a lot of refugees in our area. Their problems became her problems. I learned from my parents the power of serving. That's why I do what I do. All I know is to serve.

———

When I was young, I walked a fine line between humility and hopelessness. There were times I felt so frustrated I couldn't do more to help my parents, but there was value in understanding the limitations of the situation. It helped me accept what was happening and build relationships with negative emotions—especially fear. By developing my humility, I was able to conquer the disease of fear. The fear was ever present, but over time I realized the disease didn't have to be.

It's easy to claim victimization when you're growing up on welfare, buying groceries with food stamps, and living in Section 8 housing. I can honestly say I never did that, and I couldn't stand seeing friends and neighbors who did. They got into gang and vandalism stuff because they thought they had to rebel against a world that was keeping them down. Because of my parents, I was humble enough to know what hardship really was.

I dealt with all these problems by creating as many distractions as I could. Most of them revolved around sports. My mom was a big help with this. She got us into a whole bunch of physical activities, whatever would keep us busy and outside until it was dark. To this day, I don't like inactivity and silence. I always need to be moving.

My first sport was Taekwondo. I was in the second grade when she introduced me to the master, Bill Jones. I remember seeing a bunch of kids there doing all these moves and screaming with every attack. It was really intimidating. I was terrified of being judged. I begged my mom not to make me do it, and she let me have my way.

My dad encouraged me in his own gentle manner to try again.

One way he got me to go back was by taking me to the Iranian grocery store next to the academy. I liked the food in that store but I especially liked the owner, a Persian man named Agha Maunee. There has been a long, innate hostility between Afghans and Persians, but this man was a gem. He was a real friend to the Afghan community. He knew that very few of us had money, so he sold the food and allowed us to run tabs. I distinctly remember him writing the amounts in a small notebook, trusting that his customers would pay the money when they got it. One day I asked him why he used a pen instead of a pencil. He replied, "You can't erase ink, son." I took that to mean that he couldn't cheat his customers by changing the dollar amounts. He could screw people over if he wanted, but he was a man of humility and honor. I respected that immensely.

Since the grocery store was so close to the academy, it was easy for my dad to convince me to go back there. This time, Bill Jones came over to us wearing his blue kimono, and he put on a ninja mask. He started tumbling and poking me and joking around. We jostled a little bit and he pretended to fall. "Wow, you've got talent!" he said. He made me feel like the ultimate ninja and very comfortable. I decided to give it a try.

I can still see the smile on my dad's face. I am so grateful that he encouraged me to do something that scared me, especially since he was scared for so much of his own life.

I dove into Taekwondo with everything I had, and I got results very quickly. I got my black belt when I was still in middle school. I was starting to get noticed at tournaments. My best asset was my hands. The problem was, we couldn't afford for me to play organized sports or sign up for a lot of classes. That didn't stop my mom, or any of the other moms in our community. They found an Afghan Taekwondo instructor and set up classes in our backyards.

My success in athletics—or at least, how I defined success—gave me great confidence, but because I was young and dumb that led to a good deal of arrogance as well. I liked to challenge my instructors and would get kicked out of classes often. This was at my own house! My dad would walk up and see me sitting in the kitchen while the other boys were in the backyard breaking boards and stuff, drills I wasn't allowed to do because I was being such a dick. He would get very stern with me. "If this is how you are going to behave, perhaps we should stop creating these opportunities for you." There's nothing I hated more than disappointing my parents.

———

My life in the martial arts has been one long journey through the land of humility. After doing Taekwondo, I moved into boxing. Then I got to high school and was exposed to Jiu Jitsu. Each time I moved into a different space, I went back to being a white belt and started from the beginning. I discovered early on that you can't evolve unless you first acknowledge that there is something you don't know or can't do.

This is what I learned from my parents. For all their struggles, they were never too proud to ask for help. They were humble enough to acknowledge that they had things to overcome. Through their actions, they taught their children to believe that there is nothing our Creator will put on us that we can't bear. They surrendered to that and charged forward, constantly looking up. That was extremely humbling. I didn't pity them, I was in awe of them.

There was no sense of entitlement in our house. Our parents gave my siblings and me responsibilities. We cleaned the house and the yard, we washed the cars, we ran to the store to get my father his medications. My mom, bless her heart, was always out working somewhere. That's why I didn't rebel like my friends and vandalize property and join gangs. My siblings and I wanted to honor our parents at all times. Their humility—*our* humility—led us down a better path.

———

In time, my attention turned to soccer. We were surrounded by a lot of Afghan communities, so people set up soccer programs that represented all those towns and cities. My friends and I didn't have money for fancy uniforms, so a bunch of our moms went to local businesses like Hobby Lobby to get them to pitch in for uniforms and equipment. They also went to a secondhand store and bought used Puma cleats for around ten bucks a pair. My two cousins, Yama and Hash Jamili, helped find us inexpensive cleats and shin guards. We almost looked like real soccer players when we wore them.

The Afghan Soccer Organization hosted three or four local tournaments each year. It started when I was in elementary school, but as it got bigger we played against teams who would come from other parts of the country, like New York and Washington, D.C. Eventually that led to a big national tournament called the Afghan Cup. It would draw nearly ten thousand people to the Bay Area or Washington, D.C. You'd have intense games with big rivalries and tons of fights, and then that would be followed by music and festivities. It was the coolest thing ever. We would get a city permit, take over a park for three days, and bring in a ton of Afghan food and musicians. It was a really vivid display of the potential that sports has to unify people.

We also got to play lots of games against other teams in the area, teams that had players from every race and heritage. We were badass, man. Nobody could beat us. It was very addicting, and it made us want to learn as much we could about soccer. Any way we could get access to a pavement or flat area, you'd see kids outside playing, five or six hours a day sometimes. Yama, Sal, Mo, Jaji, Hash, Haroon, I and my brother, Yossef—our skill level grew very quickly as we prepared to rule the Bay Area. We called ourselves the Kabul Soccer Club and we played against all kinds of teams who were in "nicer" programs, and we just dominated them. It was especially sweet when we beat teams filled with rich white kids who were enjoying all the opportunities we didn't have. They were getting into all these elite tournaments and getting looked at by colleges, and we weren't getting shit. That just made us all the more determined. We knew we had to be great just to have a chance.

When I got into high school, my Afghan soccer team got invited to several adult league tournaments. We traveled to Washington, D.C., to represent the Bay Area. It was over Fourth of July weekend, and it was a blast. We raised what money we could through car washes and other fund-raising. It still wasn't a lot, so when we got to D.C. we stayed eight to a room. We spread out towels on the floor to use as pillows. It was so much fun.

As you can see, the power of sports was ingrained in my soul from a very young age. Sports were the only thing in the universe that exposed me to freedom. I believed I could do anything and be whatever I wanted when I was playing. A lot of friends and cousins of mine didn't have that feeling. They were too afraid of rejection or failure to get involved in organized sports. That robbed them of their self-worth. I never had that problem. I looked around and said, "Fuck that. I'm better than these white dudes. I'm better than these Black dudes. I'm better than these Mexicans."

Almost all of my soccer friends had the same mind-set as me. They were supportive all the way. Why were we so different from so many of our friends? Yes, we had a lot of ability, but what really differentiated us was our support systems. I was close with my mom's three brothers, Ehsan, Mohammad, and Tony. They were the committee inside our home that ruled on any big decision. If my siblings and I could get them to approve something, my parents probably would go along with it. They were sons of the general, too, and they had that kind of presence about them. Their approval was very important to me.

Most of all, I was lucky that my parents were so supportive of all my curiosity. A lot of parents around us were telling their kids they had to go right to work after they graduated from high school. It wasn't just because the family needed the money—though that was often true; it was because the parents couldn't imagine that their children could achieve truly big things in America. They didn't think their kids could become doctors or lawyers or entrepreneurs. It was like those things didn't exist for them.

Not my folks. They wanted us to dream big dreams and chase every one.

Looking back, it's clear to me that my dad's mental problems started before he even came to America. Manic depression, bipolarism, schizophrenia—he had a little bit of everything. When he felt destructive, he would seal himself into his own world.

A big reason for that was because from the time he was young, my father was told not to feel these negative emotions. He thought of them as weaknesses. I believe this was the whole root of his problems—and the root of problems for so many people around the world. When you don't have the proper sense of humility, you fool yourself into believing you should be able to overcome these things.

I can't say I was embarrassed about my father's condition because no one outside our house knew about it. My dad would never have an episode in public. I never worried about people finding out because I didn't quite comprehend myself that something was wrong. I thought it was normal. I was actually more embarrassed about our financial situation, being on Medi-Cal and food stamps. Little did I know just how many people around us were in the same situation.

Sad, isn't it? There is so much shame attached to these things. That's a big problem in the world today. I think we need more humility and less shame. If everybody in my family had been more open with each other, we could have been there for each other and walked around the neighborhood without fear of being judged. Back then, though, that fear of judgment was very real.

I was very, very lucky in one important respect: for all their challenges, my parents were humble enough to admit their vulnerability and ask for help. They could have tamped down all their problems out of embarrassment. My dad would often say how grateful he was to live in a country with a system that provided him with the help he needed. That had a huge impact on me. I learned that if you need help, you should be humble enough to ask for it.

The Game Plan: Jake Shields Fights with Humility

In 2007, I started spending more time at a gym in the Bay Area called Fairtex. This was the primary spot for local guys who were training to be high-level Mixed Martial Arts fighters. I discovered Fairtex when I was still in college and was mesmerized by the vibe in there. MMA was still developing as a sport, but it was growing fast, and I wanted to ride the wave.

One of the top fighters in that training group was Jake Shields. He was already well established as one of the world's best mixed martial artists. Jake was about halfway through an epic fifteen-fight win streak when I met him. And yet, from the start I could tell he was eager to learn, hungry to get better, and humble enough to understand just how much he needed to learn.

Jake had a regular crew that he trained and sparred with, but it wasn't easy to find new blood. When we first started working out he became eager to form a deeper relationship. Most of the guys got beat up a couple of times and never came back. But I kept coming. Jake was really good at grappling, but I was the better stand-up boxer. I was also dependable and loyal, which was just as important.

The more I trained and spoke with Jake, the more I realized how much we were aligned. We were both brutally honest about our deficiencies, and we respected each other's strengths. There was no ego involved, just an instant level of comfort. He told me he thought he could use my help, even though I had never trained or coached anyone in an official capacity. I committed to him, largely because I wanted to learn as much as I could from him.

Jake does not have the typical background you would expect from an MMA champion. He was born in 1979 on a farm about an hour outside of Nashville, Tennessee. At the time his parents and two older brothers were part of a large hippie commune. (Jake's middle name is Sequoyah, a legendary Cherokee tribal leader who lived in the early nineteenth century.) When Jake was very young the family moved to Mountain Ranch, California, in the Sierra Nevada. Jake was homeschooled until he was in junior high school and raised as a vegetarian. The Shieldses' house sat at the end of a long dirt road on the rim of the Jesus Maria Canyon. In order to see other kids, Jake and his two older brothers had to go on a long forty-five-minute hike through the canyon. They grew up climbing those mountains, biking through the woods, and playing in caves.

Jake's first love was wrestling. He got into the sport when he was about nine years old and later became a two-time junior college All-American at Cuesta College. That earned him a scholarship to San Francisco State University. Jake soon fell into Jiu Jitsu. He also started working out with Chuck Lidell, who was the first mainstream superstar for MMA. Jake's parents weren't crazy about their son becoming a professional fighter, but once they could see how committed Jake was, they supported him completely. His dad became his manager and his mom helped keep them both organized. It was a family affair.

You might ask how a kid who grew up living off the land and surrounded by hippies became one of the most lethal MMA fighters on the planet. Jake's father, Jack, had a lot to do with that. He was a former Green Beret who was once deployed to fight in Iran. Jack was a physically fit, highly competitive man, and he raised his son with that mentality. Along with wrestling, Jack showed Jake and his brothers the basics of martial arts, which Jack learned while serving in the military. Through his father, Jake came to understand that the sport of wrestling wasn't about trying to hurt someone. It was about discipline and competitiveness. That gave Jake an air of humility as he moved up the MMA ranks. He wasn't in the fight game so he could dominate other people. His purpose was to become the best version of himself, limitations and all.

This is what a lot of people misunderstand about professional fighters. It's not like they're walking around thinking they're bad-asses. Most of the time when a fighter steps into the ring, he is extremely nervous. He feels vulnerable. That's part of what fighters are seeking when they compete. If they're not scared, it's not real to them.

Training for a big fight is hard, lonely work, so every encouraging word goes a long way. In finding the right words to move Jake along, I learned that I have a gift for giving people positive energy, especially when they are feeling afraid. It was my job to bring new ideas into our sessions. I would do some research, look for things that I thought were worth trying, and work them into our sessions. In return Jake would bounce his thoughts off me. My primary message was that there was more to fighting than just overpowering your opponent. I felt Jake had to get smarter and more technically proficient. Jake's strengths were wrestling and Jiu Jitsu, so it was up to me to develop him into a more well-rounded fighter. Normally there are two aspects to stand-up fighting: attacking and defending. Jake and I developed a model where you defend yourself by attacking. That way Jake could keep utilizing his strengths while still leaving himself protected. This was a very innovative approach but it worked extremely well.

It takes a lot of balls for a guy who has basically never trained anyone to start telling a world champion what he needs to change, but Jake was humble enough to consider what I was trying to say. I brought my own healthy dose of humility to the task. I wasn't trying to hide the fact that I didn't have a lot of experience as a coach, but I did have other experiences that Jake didn't have, and the lessons I gleaned from those could help make him better.

The bond that Jake and I established through months of training was invaluable on fight nights. It's hard not to be rattled when you step into that octagon with thousands of people in the arena. Knowing he had someone like me and our teammate Gilbert Melendez who were confident and relaxed helped ease his nerves. It wasn't false confidence, either. We knew how hard we had worked to prepare for that moment. My specialty was getting inside his head to keep him cool and efficient.

Even as Jake became this wildly successful, rich, famous MMA icon, he has remained one of the most genuinely humble people I've ever known. I've seen Jake in the gym during a break talking to one of the other fighters, and I'm talking no-name hobbyist guys off the street just there for a workout, and he's listening to them and considering their advice like they're world champions. He genuinely believes there is something he can learn from everyone.

Like me, Jake has never been handed anything. He finds value in every experience, good and bad. He has turned down a lot of money from potential sponsors because he doesn't want his ass kissed all the time. I've always respected that about him and tried to operate my life and business the same way.

I went through a tough experience with Jake where I really learned about his competitor's heart. It happened in the fall of 2011, when Jake's father died unexpectedly three weeks before Jake was supposed to partake in a huge UFC fight in New Orleans against Jake Ellenberger. Jake and his dad were extremely close. When I heard the news, I assumed there was no way Jake would go through with the fight, but he never wavered. He told me his dad would have wanted him to compete. It was a tough three weeks of training camp. All of us had heavy hearts, but Jake trained as hard as always.

Unfortunately, the fight did not go well. In the first few minutes, Jake got hot-kneed and was knocked down. This happened sometimes in training so it was nothing he couldn't handle, but the referee moved in quickly and stopped the fight. Under normal circumstances he shouldn't have lost, but I was more impressed that Jake still wanted to train his ass off, get in the cage, and take this guy on. It was the first time I truly realized what I was coaching. There was not going to be anything that was going to come between Jake and competing, which is exactly how his father had raised him. From that point on, I knew Jake would be successful in whatever he wanted to do, because he goes all out for what he believes in. He was able to surrender to the things he couldn't control and still press forward.

I've learned so much by watching Jake Shields operate. He has zero interest in being famous. He simply loves what he does. He'll capitalize on his fame sometimes, but he's not going to go out of his way to do photo shoots or get his hair fluffed out or jump on every podcast. The guy is committed to his truth, and that is all about competing. He is the epitome of humility because he still wants to keep learning and getting better. This is why we connect so well. We are always pushing each other.

People ask him all the time if he's ever been challenged by random dudes, but it's actually never happened. Jake is a competitor and a craftsman, not a bully. He doesn't go around looking for fights. He is now retired from MMA, but he's still competing in Jiu Jitsu tournaments. He's dominating, of course.

Don't get me wrong. Jake knows just how good he is. He carries a strong confidence that all great athletes need. Athletes in general, and fighters in particular, tend to be afraid when they step into the ring or between the lines. The difference between them and most other people is they push through that fear and still give it their best.

I believe that Jake would say that in the years we've known each other I have never changed, either. I deal with a lot of famous athletes, CEOs, and millionaires, but I treat everyone equally and with respect. That has become an integral part of my own personal game plan, which Jake holds me accountable to in much the same way I do for him. Through my work and friendship with Jake Shields, I have learned that a humble fighter packs a powerful punch.

CHAPTER THREE

COMMUNITY

I was fortunate that I went to diverse schools. My middle school was about a third white. The rest were Mexicans, Blacks, Pacific Islanders, Filipinos, and the like. The students generally came from lower-middle-class backgrounds. I don't remember experiencing a lot of racism. When my family went out to dinner I'd see puzzled faces from people who were thinking, *What are they doing here?* To be fair, though, my family was a little different. We wouldn't go to an outdoor event with a little picnic basket. We'd show up with a slaughtered cow and then eat it like a bunch of barbarians. I can see how that might attract a little attention.

My two closest friends from elementary to high school were white: Dave Tollefson, a linebacker on the football team, and Trent Holsman, a big-time swimmer. Both were a year older than me, and because they were such great athletes, I looked up to them. Even at a young age, Trent was incredibly dedicated as a swimmer.

This dude had zero social life. He taught me what it means to be the best and the price you have to pay to get there.

Trent and Dave became like my brothers, but it definitely created a weird vibe with my Afghan friends—my core community. We called ourselves the Afghan Empire, and we were a closed-off group. My friends weren't confrontational, but they would make these little comments here and there about Trent and Dave. We'd talk about going somewhere and someone would crack, "Oh, T probably can't come because he wants to hang out with the white boys." Or, "I don't know if T is gonna want to play on this team. It's an Afghan team." They were meant to be jokes, but I always understood there was a deeper meaning there, and I didn't appreciate it.

Those wiseass comments reflected a self-defeating mind-set that says if you are interested in trying new things or growing as a person, then somehow you are betraying your community by "acting white." This became more problematic later on as I continued to push myself into situations that made me uncomfortable but I knew would lead me to my purpose. I resented the attitudes my Afghan friends showed, but I never let them stop me.

My high school was an interesting place, to say the least. It was kind of like Disneyland, only meaner. You had all these different "worlds" in separate sections of the "park." You had Blacks, Mexicans, Filipinos, Afghans, and such, with everyone setting up shop in their own corners of the campus. The only place where all those groups really mingled was on the football team. That could make things awkward when fights broke out. There was like this mini war going on for a while. I remember one time seeing a nasty fight between a Black guy and an Afghani student. Other people joined in, and this Black guy who was on the football team said to me, "We're family on the team, bro, but blood is thicker than water. I get it if you gotta ride with your boys."

I remember one day these guys started ganging up on me and a few of my Afghan buddies. A fight broke out right on the quad. I grabbed and punched whoever I could, and out of the corner of my eye I saw Trent and Dave sprinting my way. They jumped in and started fighting. They were flinging these little punks into walls and onto the pavement. Believe me, my boys were impressed. Later on they were laughing how these white dudes saved the Afghan Empire!

Thanks to my status as an athlete, I felt very comfortable when I got to Ygnacio Valley High School. I was made a starter on the varsity soccer team as a freshman, but I was quickly switching my emphasis to football. My high school had a freshman football coach named Mike Ivankovich. He was a legend in the Bay Area. He knew I was a good soccer player, but mostly I was just a good overall athlete. He saw what a strong kicker I was, so he used me on kickoffs. I almost always booted the ball through the end zone for a touchback.

I hope I don't sound arrogant when I talk about my success as an athlete. My definition of success is the confidence I gained and the things I learned about myself by playing sports. Most people define success by how much money they make or how far they get in their careers. I believe our definition of success should evolve every day. It should boil down to the ability to embrace where you are today. We should be careful about attaching ourselves to things that aren't really ours, things we can't take to our graves. So it wasn't my athletic accomplishments that made me successful but rather the feelings I got from them. That meant sacrifice and pain. If I didn't sweat and bleed and hurt when I climbed into bed at night, then I didn't feel successful.

Coach Ivankovich asked if I wanted to get deeper into football and play more positions. At first I said no, because I was dedicated to soccer, but when he pushed the issue I told him I liked the idea of rushing the passer. The next day, the coach came up to me at football practice, told me where to stand, and said, "Don't let these guys stop you." On the very first snap, I got to the quarterback. I became a backup defensive lineman on the junior varsity, rotating into the game every other series, but my main position was kicker.

To be honest, I thought I was good enough to start on the varsity. Confidence was never a problem for me. But I could see there was a lot of politics in play, especially with respect to the parents. My folks didn't know how to play that game. I figured out early on that if I was going to become a starter on this team, I would really have to earn it. That would become a theme for the rest of my life.

Playing on the varsity track and soccer teams as a freshman meant I could hang out with the older guys in school—the cool guys. My heart was in soccer, but the football program was much more respected. It just so happened that when I got to the high school, a bunch of very motivated former high school and college players joined the coaching staff. The team had never won big before, but now there was a movement to make it happen. I wanted to be a part of that. Soccer was fun, but football quickly became a brotherhood.

So it was that the football team at Ygnacio Valley High School became the first community outside of my family and our Afghan relatives and neighbors that I really felt a part of. It was an amazing feeling. By becoming a member of this dedicated, diverse group of football players, I felt invincible. That's what being part of a strong community can do for you. I have been working to build, grow, and protect my own community ever since.

———

The coaches at my high school were more influential than the principal or teachers. They had a green light from all the parents to beat our asses if we deserved it. That team was a real family, man. We'd travel to camps and sleep on gym floors together. I would roll with these older guys downtown, making a bunch of noise and trying to meet girls.

The more we won, the more the town—the greater community— rallied around us. That brought an even greater sense of responsibility. The football coaches instilled in us the importance of sticking up for each other, of doing well in school, of carrying ourselves in a way that would represent the program with class. It was almost like those coaches were an extension of my parents, Coach Ivankovich most of all.

I especially loved how diverse the team was. In soccer, it was always the Afghans versus the whites or the Mexicans, but there are so many more people on a football team that you can't limit yourselves that way. We had a Thursday night pasta dinner every week where we were forced to socialize with our teammates and meet their families. I would go into different homes and see various lifestyles and etiquettes. It was very enlightening.

My big break came early in my junior year. I was a really good linebacker and defensive end, but the guys ahead of me were badass. One of the starters got banged up toward the end of the game, so my coach sent me in. It was like in the movie *Rudy*. Everyone knew how hard I had worked and how much it meant for me finally to get in a game. When I snapped on my helmet and sprinted onto the field, they were as geeked up as I was.

Sure enough, just like in the movie, the other team snapped the ball. On the first play I sacked the quarterback. The entire bench rushed onto the field and swarmed me. Guys were tackling me, slapping my shoulder pads, punching me in the gut. I couldn't even feel good about the play because I was so caught up in how good they felt about *me.*

Silly as it sounds, that play changed my life. For the first time in my life, I felt like I really and truly belonged to a real community. It didn't happen because of special connections or because my parents played politics with the coaches. It was because I worked my ass off so that when my chance came, I'd be ready. Sometimes you wonder if anyone really understands how hard you are working. When my teammates reacted like that, it validated everything I had done. From that moment on, I was absolutely obsessive about sports. Besides my family, it became the most important force in my life.

By then the team had become a real point of pride for our

town. I remember at that time *Varsity Blues* was very popular, and we all aspired to be like the guys in that movie. As players, we were super committed to our team and to each other year-round. Our junior year ended with us losing in the state semi championship game. We sat around and cried for two hours. As sad as that was, it was a major bonding experience. All of my family was at that game. I was so happy that they got to see the type of unity I had formed with this group. It was crushing to see the seniors lose their last game. The juniors made a pact that we would work even harder in the off-season and win the championship for those guys.

I knew senior year would be big for me, so I basically lived in the gym. I loved busting my ass and getting results. When I was a junior I got my first stretch marks, and all the guys on the team went nuts for me. My dad would drop me off at Gold's Gym and I would basically spend the whole day there. When I wasn't in the gym, I carried around with me gallons of water mixed with protein. As a result, I put on sixteen pounds of muscle.

When the season came, I balled out. I played defensive end and outside linebacker on defense and wingback on offense. I also kicked and punted. I broke the school's sack record that year and at the end of the season I was named most improved player. We won the state championship for the first time in twenty-five years.

Because of my place on the team, I was invited to participate in a lot of different social groups around the school. Trent, who was older than me, had been student body president, so when I became a senior I decided to run. I put together this big campaign and won decisively. I got to be very close with the principal and vice principal but, to be honest, I was a pain in the ass to most of my teachers. I didn't do anything that would get me expelled or anything, but I liked to test people.

By that point I had started to think about my life after high school. I knew I would need football to help me get into college, because I was not the same type of performer in the classroom. Looking back, I believe I had an undiagnosed learning disability, probably attention deficit disorder. It was very difficult for me to concentrate, and I was always afraid to speak up in class because I was afraid of being judged. My answer was to hustle my way through and barely pass. I graduated with a 2.3 grade point average.

It's a shame, because with my football ability and economic status, I probably would have gotten a scholarship somewhere if I had had better grades. It was hard to look back on that and know that if I had been honest about my troubles with learning and inability to retain information, I could have gotten the help I needed to get better results. That was a mistake I swore never to repeat again.

I got some notice from an assistant coach at Cal. He came to a playoff game and saw me get two sacks and knock out the punter. I allowed myself to dream big dreams. My family, which was always on the move, was holed up in this little apartment. I wanted a better lifestyle, but I was pessimistic that football would be my ticket. I don't know if it was because of my grades or the fact that I didn't have rich parents, but I saw all these guys from other schools getting Division I offers, and I was getting nothing, even though I knew I was better than they were. I started thinking about joining the military and becoming a Navy SEAL or joining the Air Force Special Operations Command. I even started wearing an Air Force shirt around school. When one of my coaches asked me why, I told him about my intentions. "Why would you do that, T?" he said. "You could play college ball."

That's all he said, but it stuck. I just needed someone to believe in me the way I believed in myself. Finally, I got a phone call from Mike Darr, who was the defensive coordinator at Los Medanos Junior College. This was the phone call—and the man—who would change my life. "I hear you're thinking about not playing football anymore," he said. I told him it was true, and he invited me to come to campus and meet him.

I went on a visit with my high school teammate Sione Finau, who was one of my good friends from childhood. An assistant coach drove us around on a golf cart and showed us the campus and the athletic facilities. For guys who came up the way we did, we thought it was the most impressive thing we had ever seen. They had a locker room! With showers! I know it was just a juco, but to us it felt like pay dirt.

They took us in to meet Coach Darr. He was one of the top defensive minds in the country, at any level. Coach Darr told us he believed we could be Division I players if we developed physically and shored up our academics. As was the case with my high school coach, I knew Coach Darr would take care of me as long as I did my part.

I had an awesome freshman season, and I did much better in the classroom, pulling out a 3.6 grade point average. I caught the eye of a bunch of Division I coaches who came to LMC primarily to watch other players. Coach Darr and his staff really worked the phones for me and let other schools know I was drawing interest. That's when Fresno State said they wanted me to come on a recruiting visit. I was worried that they wouldn't take me because my height was six-foot-one, so I stuffed a pair of socks into each shoe in order to make me look two inches taller. My linebacker coach, Ed Hall, insisted I wear a suit on that trip. "This is a job interview," he said. "You need to dress for it."

Fresno State had a lot of appeal for me. It was close to my family in the Bay Area, and the football program had achieved national prominence. Dave Tollefson rode with me in his 1985 Buick Regal. I knew they were going to weigh me so I chugged water the whole ride up. Before we went inside, Dave made me do a bunch of neck raises so I would look jacked up. I met Pat Hill, the head coach, on my visit. "We're a football team, and we like to hit," he said. "Watching your highlight film, it looks to me like you like to hit, too." He spoke to me for a few minutes and then offered to drive me around campus on a golf cart. I told him it wasn't necessary. Because the way he spoke to me, I immediately knew I wanted to play for this man. We shook hands, and then one of his assistants took me straight to the admissions office. I was ready to join a new community.

The Game Plan: Marshawn Lynch, Community Warrior

I got to know Tom Cable very well when he was the head coach of the Oakland Raiders from 2008 to 2010. After he was let go, Cabes latched on with the Seattle Seahawks as their offensive line coach and run game coordinator. In late 2010, he called me about a young running back who had recently joined the Seahawks but was having trouble reaching his potential. The guy's name was Marshawn Lynch.

Cabes felt like Marshawn had some inner struggles but that if he could break through these knots and get comfortable in his truth, he could be one of the greatest running backs of all time. I was a big football fan, so I knew exactly who Marshawn Lynch was. He had been drafted by the Buffalo Bills with the twelfth overall pick in the 2007 NFL Draft, but things did not work out for him in Buffalo. Marshawn had a bunch of injuries that kept him from breaking through on the field, and he also had some issues off the field, most notably when he was suspended by the NFL for three games after he pled guilty to a misdemeanor gun charge. The Bills traded Marshawn to Seattle one month into the 2010 season.

I had read some unflattering things about Marshawn, but I never believe anything I see in the media because you just don't know who has been pushing that narrative. If anything, I gravitate toward people who get bad press. My default assumption is that these must be very principled human beings who held deep conviction in order to pursue their own authentic paths, right or wrong. I've built my community with those kinds of people. I'm pretty strong-willed myself, so I can relate.

Needless to say, I said I'd be happy to meet with him. "What do you want me to tell him?" I asked.

"You'll figure it out," Cabes replied.

I told Cabes he could give Marshawn my info. Within a couple of hours, I got a call from a 510 area code. Marshawn and I spoke briefly on the phone and agreed that we would meet at my office at Empower the next morning at nine o'clock.

He showed up at eight thirty. Right off the bat, that scored major points with me. I really respect people who appreciate the value of time. And in that vein, I decided not to waste his. "Why does Cabes want me to meet with you?" he asked.

I smiled and said, "He told me you're scared of pain and Muslims."

We both laughed. The rules of engagement had been set.

Was that rude or bold or stupid of me to say? Hardly. Whenever I meet someone, my first goal is to lower the waterline and create a level of comfort, which can be challenging considering these are uncomfortable conversations. I always want my teammates to know that we can laugh about anything. So I am perfectly honest from the first moment in hopes my new teammate will be as well. If it works, great. If not, that's okay, too. There have been too many occasions when I hesitate and strategize and communicate in ways that are not true to myself. Those usually do not go well. But when I am my authentic self, I'm at a near 100 percent hit rate with relationships.

My intent was to set that tone so Marshawn could be the same way with me. I told him I wanted to understand him because someone in his position had a big responsibility to the world. I told him I wanted to help him expose his true purpose as a man first and a football player second.

"I know you've made some mistakes," I said. "I read all these things about you, and Cabes tells me you've had some hiccups. I think you're misunderstood."

I told Marshawn about my own experiences with hiccups and how I found ways to deal with them and accept my limitations without falling into a victim's mentality. As I spoke, Marshawn put his head down and pounded his heart. "You and me are gonna be family," he said.

That was encouraging, to say the least. I shared with Marshawn some of my story and explained who I was and what I had set out to do through Empower. Then I started asking him questions, mostly about why football was so important to him. Marshawn grew up in Oakland and came from a big family. He felt a lot of pressure to deliver for them. He lived by the motto "If I'm eating, everyone's eating." That's an admirable way to think but it's also a huge responsibility—and a lot of pressure.

I didn't have to introduce the concept of community to Marshawn, because he had always lived it. His career wasn't just about being a great running back. He had bigger goals in mind. So when things didn't go his way, he wrestled with the forces he believed were aligned against him. In the end, though, he was wrestling with himself. He was stuck, and as a result he was squandering his talent.

Like so many people who come to see me, Marshawn thought we would get right into physical training. Instead we did a game plan. Marshawn had taken psychology classes at Cal and thought he didn't want therapy, but within two minutes he could see this wasn't therapy, it was a real conversation.

When he left my office, I sat at a computer and wrote out his game plan. I laid out my takeaways from the talk and established his physical goals. A few days later, he came back into Empower and we went to work. I put him through some basic physical activities, the kind of stuff you might see in a seventh-grade PE class. Push-ups, squats, military presses with medicine balls, band sprints, pull-ups, sit-ups, medicine ball squats. The works.

I asked him how many push-ups he could do. "Fifty, easy," he said. I told him, "If you can do eleven, I'll give you a thousand dollars." Needless to say, he was confused.

"What are you focusing on when you're doing push-ups?" I asked. He gave me the standard answers: his arms and his chest. "What about your hands?" I asked.

I told him to do the push-ups all the way up to his fingertips and then hold for a second at the top. He couldn't get to eleven. There was a real message in this. I was teaching him about the concept of neglect. I've seen lots of athletes, especially football players, have their careers impacted because of weak hands, which can lead to injuries. By forcing Marshawn to do push-ups on his fingers, he had no choice but to lock in on his hands. It was a moment of revelation. "Think about it," I said. "The most important thing in doing push-ups is your hands, but you never think about your hands. So what other important things in your life are you not thinking about?"

We moved on to bear crawls. His form was off, as is the case with many people when they first come to see me. My thing is, you have to do everything the exact right way if you're going to max out. Once we focus on those details, the exercises become a lot harder. And these are proud, competitive, world-class athletes. I put them in position to see their limits at the very start. That establishes humility as well as truth. Their capacity becomes exposed.

Marshawn told me he didn't want any special treatment, so I

put him in our regular noon class, which included a handful of people who worked at the tech company next door. Marshawn brought his cousin and jumped right in. I had the group running up and down a street outside of Empower. Marshawn was huffing and puffing alongside everyone else. He was bigger, stronger, and faster than everyone, so he took off ahead of them running up the Vallejo Street hill in our North Beach neighborhood. About three-quarters of the way, however, he ran out of gas. The tech folks passed him, including a woman named Tami who worked in a tech firm down the street. Marshawn sat down at the top of the hill, huffing and puffing, and said, "This ain't right. I got thirty million riding on me and these guys are busting my ass."

Tami chirped, "Then why do they call you Beast Mode?" I doubled over laughing.

That didn't happen because the other folks were in such better shape. It was because they had developed a mentality of pushing themselves as hard as they could. It was an extremely humbling experience for Marshawn. It was also another defining moment for our relationship. It made him take his training a lot more seriously and helped him understand that he had neglected the correlations between his physical capabilities and his mental and emotional ideals.

Marshawn was used to working himself past the point of exhaustion. It was my job to take him to a deeper level of mental strength, to give him tools he could call upon when he reached those moments where he felt like giving up. This is what I like to call spiritual warfare. The idea is to use a belief system that enjoys the struggle and looks for results that go much deeper than a football game. The idea wasn't to fill his head with a bunch of thoughts and philosophies but rather to *clear* his head. I wanted him to have a pure mind, the mind of a true warrior.

———

I consider it sacred when I invite someone to join my community. One day Marshawn showed up with a check. Apparently my CFO had invoiced his agency for our sessions. He thought I should get paid, but I ripped up the check and chided him for humiliating me. "You called me your brother, you said we were family," I said. "This isn't about a transaction." I wanted Marshawn to understand just where I stood. Sure, there was an upside for me to be in business with an athlete of his caliber, but remember, it was not clear at this point that he was going to turn out to be one of the best running backs in the NFL. I did it because I wanted to reach him completely.

The most important thing to understand about Marshawn is that he grew up without a father, and while his mother and grandmother were very strong presences in his life, he had a very hard time trusting men. To this day, he much prefers to take pictures with women and kids than men.

My question early on with him: Did he understand his own value? Everyone was always assigning a value to him—how many yards he ran, how many touchdowns he scored, where he was drafted. I wondered if he was capable of understanding himself outside of those designations. He came to me feeling misunderstood by others, particularly his coaches. I told Marshawn that what I wanted to know was how well *he* understood himself?

Marshawn quickly became my brother, so of course I wanted him to meet my family. I'll never forget the first time I introduced him to my dad. My dad's eyes got huge when he saw this incredible specimen come over to say hello. I had spoken so much about my dad that Marshawn was in awe of him as well. He came over to my dad, bowed his head slightly, and clasped his hand with both hands. My dad was quiet by nature, so he fell in love with someone who was physically imposing yet humble. My dad had that same powerful swag to him, like he knew he was the shit but didn't need to throw it in your face. As they posed for a picture, Marshawn held up two middle fingers for the camera. My brother, Yossef, was taking the picture and told Marshawn to cut it out, but my dad waved him off. "Let him be him," he said in Pashto. Marshawn laughed and tried to repeat those Pashto words while continuing to flip Yossef off.

Over the next two years, Marshawn lived through the whole experience with me as I watched my dad get sick and eventually die. For a long time after my dad passed, Marshawn would check up on me daily, sometimes multiple times a day. A lot of our conversations wouldn't even last a minute. Just knowing that, even with all that Marshawn had going on in his life, he still felt that love for me and wanted to make sure my family and I knew he was there for us made all the difference.

I learned a lot about Marshawn's larger intentions beyond football. When he was at Cal, he took an education class that required him to visit schools very much like the ones he attended in inner-city Oakland. That really lit a fire. He saw kids who were desperate and poor like he had been but who didn't have a fraction of his physical talent. He was determined to show them that if he could make it out of there, they could, too. He dedicated himself to becoming a warrior for his community. Before he was even drafted by the NFL, Marshawn had held his first youth football camp for kids in his old neighborhood.

This was another way in which Marshawn and I were aligned. All that talk about how he didn't trust easily turned out to be total bullshit. He trusted me right away because he understood my intentions. I didn't care about his football performance, I cared about what he wanted to do with the platform his athletic ability gave him. I never considered him a client. He was my teammate and my brother, pure and simple.

Despite his reputation with the media, you'll never find one piece of evidence that anyone in the locker room has ever complained about Marshawn. He's the best teammate, the best human being anyone can ask to play with. His problems haven't been with teammates, they've been with authority figures. That usually doesn't include his position coaches, by the way—those guys love him, because they know no one works harder or cares more about the people in that locker room. His conflicts usually come with people who are very ego-driven and try to use their authority to satisfy those egos. That's where he draws the line.

Through our conversations, I emphasized to Marshawn that while it's good to have a strong identity, your actions still have consequences. If you can live with those consequences because you've stood on principle, great, but don't act surprised when things rebound on you in a way that makes your life more difficult. Relationships are all about giving and taking, especially on a football team when you're dealing with a big locker room full of diverse personalities, and with so much of what you do being filtered by the media and into the public. What path do you follow? Wherever your moral compass points you. My purpose was to use our game plans to help Marshawn find his moral compass.

Marshawn's entire life is built around service. He wants to create opportunities for other people to fulfill their potential, whether it's sports, arts, entrepreneurship, governance, or whatever. He has built community centers through his Fam1st Family Foundation. He put a lot of energy into Beast Mode brand productions and other business ventures. He has other companies that deal with security, apparel, real estate, restaurants, and production, all of which serve to create opportunities for engagement within his community. Marshawn is very smart, especially when it comes to managing his money.

Like me, Marshawn can be brutally honest. That's a big threat to people who are trying to control him. Once again I told him that it's okay to not agree with people or to take a principled stand, but there's no reason to do it in a way that hurts you. That, however, was not his natural way of communicating. In some ways, his talent worked against him. Young people who are great athletes tend to be allowed to get away with a lot of things. In Marshawn's case, it taught him not to trust people, because he assumed everyone was there to take something from him. The longer he played, the more famous he got, the more money he made, the more protective he had to be of his own community.

———

In 2019, right around Thanksgiving, Marshawn called me and said, "Bruh, we gotta get to work." He had decided to come out of retirement and join the Seahawks as they got ready for the play-offs. He told me we only had two weeks to get him ready.

"What kind of shape are you in?" I asked.

He laughed. "I walked up two flights of stairs at the Seahawks facility and I was tired."

"Perfect," I said. "I wouldn't want it any other way. Let's ride."

He was at Empower the next morning and we started our two- and three-a-day workouts. In those two weeks we jammed in about twenty sessions. We worked on some activation stuff to get his body ready again, built up his strength and endurance, improved his cardio on Aerodyne Assault bikes, reactivated his mobility. As he went through the exercises I would punch him, kick him, elbow him, throw his body around, all to simulate what it would feel like to get pounded on a football field. The key was to get his breathing patterns correct on impact.

I also got deep into his head space. He loved football and he didn't want his career to end on a sour note. He also wanted to stay as relevant as possible for all the work he was doing to grow his brand and build his business. It made sense to me. He was healthy, he was strong, and he was hungry. What did he have to lose?

The bigger question was whether he could manage his stubbornness and repair his relationships with the Seahawks, especially with head coach Pete Carroll. I told him to go back there and be the bigger man. Don't argue, don't challenge, just accept and embrace. Maybe Pete is struggling with his own shit, too. Respect that. Marshawn took all of that to heart. He knew this was a good opportunity.

I never thought Pete and Marshawn had major problems. I told Marshawn, "Stop thinking with your heart and start thinking with your head. Let your heart do the work and let your head do the presentation." He went to Seattle and had a good meeting with Carroll. They cleared the air and set the table for his return to the field.

After two weeks of working together, I told Marshawn, "You're ready." It may seem odd to think of someone like Marshawn Lynch doubting himself, but he had assigned himself a huge task. I told him that because he had been in such optimal shape all his adult life, even when he felt a little bit off he was still way ahead of most of the other players. For a guy like him, it feels normal to be in peak condition. So if he's just a little bit off, it can hurt his confidence. I knew he was close, and he trusted me because he knew I would only tell him the truth.

The freaky part is that by then I was working as an advisor for the San Francisco 49ers. And who were the Seahawks playing that first week? The Niners, of course. I was fully transparent about everything, so everyone that week around the Niners' facility was asking me about Marshawn. I let everyone know he was serious and he was ready. In fact, he was more ready than I had ever seen him, not just physically but mentally. I had never seen him so emotionally engaged, so happy to be back playing the game he loves.

As for me, I was a bundle of nerves for the game, as you can imagine, but things turned out perfectly (for me, anyway). Marshawn ran the ball twelve times, scoring a touchdown, and the 49ers won, 26–21.

He appeared in two playoff games with the Seahawks, and while he played a limited role, he scored three more touchdowns. Powering the ball over the goal line was always where Beast Mode shined the most. (And, yes, Carroll should have given him the fucking ball on the last play of the Super Bowl against the Patriots.) The whole situation of Marshawn coming out of retirement was great for him, the Seahawks, and the NFL. At this point in his life and career, Marshawn knows how influential he is. He didn't have to go in there and cause a lot of disruption. He knows he can drive Pete crazy sometimes, but he didn't want to cause Pete any discomfort. He also understood that, as an older player, he has a responsibility to show the younger guys what being a professional is all about. Pete, meanwhile, understood the power of having that kind of leadership in his locker room. Maybe they crossed swords once in a while, but in the end the relationship worked because they could both see the benefit in it.

The major change I've seen in Marshawn is that he now takes his responsibility to himself far more seriously. He has learned his own value. Marshawn is not a person who gets taken advantage of easily. He knows how to protect himself and his community, but he tends to get overprotective and shut out people who can help him grow. He is certainly very emotional and passionate about everything he does, which is why he's my twin. We're both trying to be these tough-ass dudes but we're also very sensitive, and we've always been told not to be our natural selves.

I've used Marshawn as an illustration of community, but while his efforts to serve the community where he grew up and others around the world are admirable, that's not the kind of community I'm talking about. I'm talking about the need for all of us to build a community that will help us fulfill our potential and achieve our greater truths. It's vital to be surrounded by people who are philo-sophically aligned and who can hold us accountable. Marshawn is the glue of our community at Empower. He turns away a lot of people who want to work with me because he doesn't think we would be philosophically aligned. He protects my community as if it were his own—which, of course, it is. That's why he is my brother for life.

CHAPTER FOUR

IMPACT

I was sleeping at home while on break from my classes at Los Medanos when I got a phone call from a good friend of mine named Laura. "Are you okay?" she asked. I asked her why she wanted to know. Before she could answer, my mom opened my door because she heard my voice. She was crying. "It's a bad day," she said.

The date was September 11, 2001. I followed my mom into the living room and saw the TV coverage of the terrorist attacks. It was surreal, and it was awful.

My friend was asking me if I was okay because she knew that some people would try to blame the attacks on all Muslims. It took some time for me to process it like that, since we were all in such shock. Another buddy of mine, Jim Fultz, who was on the football team, picked me up a little later and drove us to school. We were both very quiet on the ride. Just real, real sad.

It still hadn't fully clicked with me to consider the connections between what happened and the fact that I was not only Muslim but Afghan. During lunch, some stupid shithead tried to make a joke. "I hope you're happy with what your people did," he said. I certainly didn't think it was funny. I stood up, grabbed him, slammed him on the table, and let him know in no uncertain terms how I felt about his punk-ass wisecrack. Fortunately, my friend was there to calm me down and pull me off the guy.

My buddy then took me outside and gave me good advice. "A lot of people are going to be saying stupid shit to you," he said. "But you can't fight everyone." I was really pissed, because in no way, shape, or form did I feel remotely attached in that way to what happened. I was an American college football player who grew up in California. Everything about the day was just such a nightmare, but you know what? For the most part, I didn't hear those types of comments, especially from people who knew me.

After that lunch incident, I went home to be with my family. We had lots of relatives and friends over, and my mom made a big feast. There was some good-natured joking to lighten the mood, including when my buddy referenced what had happened in the cafeteria. When everyone left, my mom got real serious with me. "I didn't want to say this in front of your friends," she said, "but this is going to be bad for our people's image. You have to use this as an opportunity to have an impact and clean our image up. You have to help educate people on who we really are."

One good thing that happened as a result of 9/11 is that it strengthened my faith. I never went to a mosque when I was grow-ing up. My parents and my grandma were my mosque. They actu-ally didn't want me to go because they didn't think anyone was more qualified to teach me than them. My grandma used to be an Islamic studies teacher in Afghanistan, and she gave us lessons when we were kids. After 9/11, I became a real student of the religion. It made me realize that if I wanted to have more of an impact and really change the way the world perceived us, I would need to be more knowledgeable about my people, my heritage, and my faith. It continues to be a deep and humbling source of strength.

———

Since that day, I have really taken that word *impact* to heart. I know it's a big part of what has driven my life's work. I want to show everyone around the world, and especially here in America, that all Afghans are not like the terrorists who flew those planes. We're scholars, we're academics, we're entrepreneurs. As horrible as 9/11 was for me, my people, and the world, it made me take an even deeper pride in my family's heritage.

The idea of what type of impact I want to have, and what that word really means, has stuck with me at every stage of my life. It has especially developed through the training work I do with clients and teammates. One of the biggest mistakes I've seen people make is tying their idea of impact to results. They are only being impactful if their actions have been properly received. I believe our impact begins with our intention. It's not about getting others to do what you want, or seeing how many likes and clicks you can get for something you posted on social media. It has to be more pure than that, and therefore more difficult. When my mom went over to Afghanistan to build private schools for women in Tora

Bora, or set up initiatives to spur local development, she wasn't trying to promote her work so the maximum number of people could know about it. She was focused on having an impact on the people in front of her.

In so many ways in life, we fall into a "results trap." It's what leads us to look elsewhere for validation. Unlike athletics, in most areas of life, your impact is not measured on a scoreboard. It exists only in your intentionality.

This is a way of thinking I often have to deconstruct when I start training a new teammate. There's a lot of quantitative analysis that goes into building up someone's body. Most times I'll start with a complete body composition analysis measuring thirty-eight different physical data points—body fat, body mass, skeletal mass, you name it. I'll also do some initial activities like fingertip push-ups and medicine ball presses, and through my game plans I collect a lot of emotional intelligence. This gives me an across-the-board baseline that I will frequently reference over the following several months.

Invariably, the client wants to know how his or her body is changing. That is supposedly what measures the impact of our work. But that is not my focus. My preference is to use the initial information as a baseline that gives me an understanding of what the person's goals are, physical, emotional, and spiritual. If someone is doing a set of push-ups, I tell him to do as many as he can, but when he stops, I always know he can do some more. Still, I almost never push that. I don't want them to do more push-ups because I told them to, or to impress me. I want them to be intentional about it. Eventually, they do push themselves to do more than they ever thought they could. That's the kind of impact I'm looking to make.

I am trying to bring that intentionality to my broader work as well. I want to have a great impact on the world, but I am always reflecting on *why* I do what I am doing at that moment. Am I doing this for myself or for others? How can I do it for others if I'm not willing to do it for myself? How can I teach clients, partners, and teammates to search for that impact that conquers fear and helps them realize their dreams?

These are ideas that would become more fully formed after I started my business. In college, however, my concept of impact was still very fuzzy and conceptual. The more I questioned what it meant, the more I searched for answers in the best place for me to find them—on a football field.

I enrolled at Fresno State in the spring of 2001 and dove right into practice. The school took in a lot of students who didn't qualify for Division I immediately out of high school, so there were a lot of kids from troubled backgrounds. It was another wonderfully diverse team, with a bunch of Blacks mixed in with Pacific Islanders and corn-bread white boys from the Valley, but I was the only Afghan American on the team. In fact, I was the only Afghan American football player in all of Division I. The idea that that would be a problem with the other players never crossed my mind. Everyone was accepting of everybody. That's what a real team is like.

For the first time in my life, I became a real student of the game. It was mind-blowing. I could tell right away that the coaches saw me as a talented player and wanted to fully exploit that. They designed all kinds of schemes for me.

My success as a college football player gave me a belief in myself that I would call upon time and again. I really needed it because a lot of bad stuff was happening with my family. By this time we had moved into like our twelfth house, and both my parents were having deep emotional problems. My dad had been taking trips to Afghanistan beginning in my senior year of high school. The visits revealed to him just how messed up things were over there. My dad grew up in the province of Kunar. He had thousands of acres of very pristine land. It included a water dam and mining mountains. On his first trip back, he discovered that all that land had been sold off by one of his own siblings. They didn't have any land deeds, so they sold it with a promissory note and never told my father about it. My dad was just heartbroken. This wasn't about lost money so much as a lost legacy. That land was the only connection he had to his family and his native country. No amount of money would have replaced that for him. He spent a year going back and forth, trying to get everything in order, and it took a lot out of him. What hurt him the most was that he was being screwed over by the same people he had once protected.

After he came home, he started having really bad panic attacks again. He would freak out over things that weren't really happening and get paranoid. He made some weird reference to the U.S. government once, like someone was out to get him. There were stretches where he would sit in his room for two or three days, sleeping and muttering to himself. He didn't want to be alive, much less awake.

I understood what was happening, but I was so busy with football that I didn't feel like I could help. I didn't know how to have an impact on him. I tried to talk to him about what was going on with him, but he never wanted us to worry about him. "Oh, it's just my medication," he would say. He didn't have any more hospitalizations, but my home was a very messed-up place to be. I did everything I could to stay out of it while Dina and Yossef busted their asses to keep things together at home.

All of this was hard for my mom as well. She was the one who encouraged my dad to bring as many relatives as he could to America. A lot of my aunts married men who, it seemed to me, just wanted their inheritances. My dad didn't want those guys around, but he also didn't have the courage to say anything to them. He would just keep quiet, which led him to blame himself even more. That's why he pushed me so hard to be as competitive as I could be. It's like he sensed he would need that from me someday.

I wanted to have a positive impact at home so badly, but I didn't know how. So I did my best to have an impact on my football team. If nothing else, I knew that would make my parents and siblings proud. That was a big part of my motivation to succeed in sports. When I was in high school, I would do something great in a football game, and the next morning my mom would see my name in the newspaper and feel proud of me. I got a lot of awards and varsity letters, and then I got elected student body president. It helped them realize that they were really doing a great job as parents.

The state championship we won my senior year of high school was as great for them as it was for me. My success as a football player expanded their social circles by getting them invited to all these team parties and school functions. I saw my mom make friends with other moms, finally connecting with people outside of our tight-knit Afghan community. It was a powerful lesson for me that the impact of sports could extend well beyond the players and coaches on that team. I would carry that lesson to college and beyond.

———

Ever since I was very young, I've had a fascination with martial arts. A lot of kids from my youth soccer teams boxed and did Taekwondo. It was fun hitting all the clubs and just learning what was out there.

When I got to Fresno State, my interest in martial arts skyrocketed. Immediately I could see the parallels between those pursuits and football. I could utilize all the technical capabilities I developed through boxing, Jiu Jitsu, wrestling, and Taekwondo and apply them to football moves like coming off the edge and rushing the passer. I would need that advantage because I was going up against some of the best offensive linemen in Division I football. The more I applied what I was learning in martial arts, the more success I was having in the trenches.

Once I saw that bit of daylight, I became obsessed with giving myself that competitive edge. I dove in completely, knowing that I was using skills and knowledge that none of my competitors were using. All those hours of grappling, wrestling, and boxing came together and I developed a true fighting approach to my mission.

I thought back to all those times when I grappled with guys

who were subduing me with arm bars and utilizing my strength, force, and power against me. There were so many times when I was thinking, *Man, I must be doing something wrong. This guy is half my size, and he almost blew out my shoulder.* I had a lot of friends on the Fresno State wrestling team, and I loved watching them in action. They understood the concept of leverage, and they had grit like I had never seen.

In an effort to further develop my skills, I made occasional trips to Southern California to train with my longtime teammate and close friend Jarrod Kwity, who later with Jake Shields gave me my black belt in Jiu Jitsu. That motivated me to continue diversifying and developing my martial arts education. I would go to UFC events and make friends with guys who were competing on the most prestigious stage for the fighting arts.

It turned out Fresno was a great place to get the martial arts bug. Some of the local casinos were just starting to host big-time MMA fights. A lot of fighters came through town to train. They would show up at the gyms, which gave me a chance to spar with some of the best MMA fighters in the world. I felt like I was getting pretty good at it. When I would go home, I would put out the word and find another local MMA facility. At the time, there weren't nearly as many as there are now, but wherever they were, I found them.

During a 2002 trip to see one of these fights in Vegas, I met a top fighter named David Terrell. I told him that I was a football player at Fresno State who had done some training. He invited me to train with him in the Bay Area, and on my next trip home I worked out with him at his school in Santa Rosa.

I was a nobody on the fight scene, compared to these guys, but I did have one very important piece of street cred: cauliflower ears. My ears might look nasty to you, but to a trained fighter they are a thing of beauty. It happens as a result of repeated blunt trauma. The cartilage cracks and the body replaces it with a natural fluid. It's a deformity, basically. It got really bad because every day after football practice I would go straight to Jiu Jitsu. It doesn't hurt too bad when your ear breaks, but it does get sensitive, like an inflamed mosquito bite. It's definitely a point of pride in my world.

I got to be good friends socially with David, and I met a bunch of his fighter friends. One night we were in a club and he pointed to a guy and said, "You see that pretty boy over there? He may look like a frat kid, but he's a total badass and you guys should train together." The guy's name was Jake Shields. David introduced us and we had a good hang.

As you can tell, when I get passionate about something, I go all in. My life was spent training, watching other guys train, and going to fights. It occurred to me at some point that while all these guys were training together and sparring with each other, nobody was coaching them. MMA wasn't considered a real sport back then, more like a hobby. But it was interesting to see all these various disciplines converging in the gym. You'd have guys like me who excelled at boxing working out with dudes who were awesome wrestlers or specialized in Jiu Jitsu. We would all just coach each other about what we knew. It started to dawn on me that if we ever put all of this together, we could craft something really cool.

So I had a lot going on when I got to Fresno State—my family issues, the shadow of 9/11, my football career, a budding interest in martial arts and ultimate fighting—all while trying to do a decent enough job in school and maintain my own sanity. I didn't quite know it yet, but I was moving toward a mindspace where somehow, some way, I was going to have a major impact on the world. I was using martial arts as a way to fine-tune those instincts and optimize my capacities. I thought I was training and fighting, but I was actually gaining leverage. Years later, I would partner with a teammate who also wanted to have an impact. Her means of delivering it wasn't through fighting but through serving.

The Game Plan: Tulsi Gabbard's Impact Through Service

When Tulsi Gabbard was growing up in Hawaii, her family owned a small, health-conscious home-style deli. Oftentimes, there would be food left over at the end of the day, so Tulsi and her family would fix some plates and deliver them to homeless people. Five minutes before she got there, these people had no idea where their next meal was coming from. Now they were holding a wonderful plate of food, brought by a heavenly angel disguised as a young girl.

In those moments, Tulsi felt a small but profound stirring. Doing something for others made her happy, especially when she expected nothing in return. In her small but important way, she was making an impact. It made her want to do it again.

Tulsi grew up to find an outlet for her desire to serve through politics and the military. Passionate about protecting the environment and precious resources such as water, Tulsi was elected to the Hawaii legislature at the age of twenty-one. Then came 9/11. The attacks lit an immense fire in Tulsi's soul, and she was determined to do her part in bringing justice to the people who had attacked our country. So she enlisted in the Hawaii Army National Guard, and in 2004 she left her seat in the state legislature and volunteered to deploy with her unit to serve in a medical unit for a one-year tour in Iraq.

Tulsi's actions stemmed not only out of a desire to serve her country and her fellow man but also her God. Tulsi is a practicing Hindi who subscribes to the Gaudiya Vaishnava branch of Hinduism, which focuses on the practice of Bhakti Yoga, which means dedicating one's life to loving service to God. Tulsi also practices Karma yoga, which is often called the "yoga of action." The main spiritual text she studies is the *Bhagavad Gita*, which teaches in one passage, "Your work is your responsibility, not its result. Never let the fruits of your actions be your motive. Nor give in to inaction."

As she was growing up, Tulsi also developed a deep interest in martial arts. She first learned Taekwondo but got to a point where her family could not afford to pay for the classes. So she flipped through the martial arts section of the yellow pages to find something else she could learn and ended up taking free capoeira lessons in a local park. Eventually, she became a capoeira instructor, volunteering to teach kids at the local Boys & Girls Club, and later sharing capoeira with her fellow service members when she was deployed to Iraq. Like me, Tulsi was drawn not just to the physical moves in martial arts but the ethos of discipline and balance. Combined with a lifelong plant-based diet, this holistic approach to her life has kept her grounded through incredible successes and some very challenging times.

When she was deployed to Iraq for a twelve-month tour beginning in 2004, she was assigned to work in a medical unit at a camp forty miles north of Baghdad. She kept to her plant-based diet, which made it challenging for her to get the nourishment she needed and led to some good-natured teasing from her fellow soldiers. The camp she and her fellow soldiers were based out of was the target of indirect mortar fire on almost a daily basis—so much that it was nicknamed "Mortaritaville." When the sirens would go off, Tulsi would take cover in a concrete bunker. There was a big sign by one of the main gates that read, "Is today the day?"

In that situation, a fear of death is not some irrational, far-off abstraction but a daily reality. If you're looking to conquer the disease of fear, "Mortaritaville" is as good a place as any.

What's amazing about all of this is that Tulsi is by nature an introvert. She was so shy about talking to strangers when she was growing up that her younger sister frequently had to step in and speak for her. Yet she set aside her fears and worked to fulfill her dharma, her purpose. When she got back home from her second deployment, this time to Kuwait, Tulsi ran for a seat on the Honolulu City Council and won. Two years later, in 2012, she got elected to the U.S. House of Representatives, becoming the first Hindu woman and one of the first female combat veterans ever to serve in Congress. Seven years later, Tulsi made yet another unconventional decision, this one the most astounding of all. She decided to run for president. Of the United States.

———

I don't follow politics that closely, but I had been impressed with Tulsi over the years, and I watched her presidential campaign with some interest. I knew she had spent extensive time in combat in the Middle East, and I thought she was proposing some radical, creative solutions to some very complex problems, particularly with regard to foreign policy. Regardless of whether I agreed with all her policy ideas, I've always been drawn to anyone who's a nonconformist. That's something I can really relate to.

I mentioned my positive impression of Tulsi to a friend of mine one day and he showed me a video of her being interviewed on a talk show. The hosts were giving her a hard time. There was something about her answers that bothered me—not the content necessarily, but the way she was expressing herself. I suspected that instead of saying what she really thought, she was trying to anticipate land mines that were four and five steps ahead, and the hosts were eager to bully her into making a bad mistake.

I took out my phone, found Tulsi's official Instagram account, and sent her a direct message. She had no reason to know me, but I wrote, "Anything I can do to be of service and help you, I'm in." I figured that would be the end of it, but a short while later I got a return message. At that time her sister was managing all of Tulsi's social media accounts, and when she received my DM she passed along my information to Tulsi. Tulsi read the ESPN profile that was linked to my bio and was drawn in to my story. She had worked with personal trainers before who were great at promising six-pack abs, but did that really strengthen her? It's like a doctor who only treats the symptom and not the actual problem.

Tulsi could also relate to some of my own experiences in the Middle East. It dovetailed with her own worldview of foreign policy, which is rooted in the effort to gain an understanding of people whom society says you shouldn't be talking to—people who have been labeled the "enemy." It takes courage to sit down with that person and try to choose a diplomatic path to peace, rather than a military one. Tulsi and I had both tried that.

She told her sister to reply to my DM and set up a time for us to talk. It so happened that they were coming to LA in a few days. We decided to get together.

Did you ever meet someone for the first time and instantly feel like you've known them for your entire life? That's what it was like when Tulsi and I met for coffee in the lobby of her hotel. There was no small talk to be had. She told me all about her life and her faith and her vision for the future. I told her about my work in performance development and entrepreneurship. That was the start of what she now calls the "T and T" show. We were like brother and sister. We also discovered we have the same birthday, which of course was no coincidence.

As a member of Congress, Tulsi worked in a culture that was filled with transactional relationships. You do something for me, I do something for you. I am used to this expectation from elite athletes and business executives. They come in with a dose of skepticism. Like, what can anybody give me that I don't already have? Yet, there I was, asking Tulsi four words she rarely hears: "How can I help?"

How do I keep my intentions pure? For starters, I've never set money as an ultimate goal. I know if I'm good at what I do, the money will come, but that's not what drives me to my dharma. My life's work is to try to empower people who are trying to have an impact. The best way for me to learn is to teach them. In Tulsi's case, I wanted to learn everything I could about this person who was trying to change the world. I was amazed that she had the balls to run for president as a thirty-nine-year-old Hindu woman from Hawaii. She knew it was a long shot, that she would be exposed and her brand would be manipulated. Yet she was still willing to put all of that on the line.

Most of all, we connected because we both have a deep spiritual center and devotion to our faiths. Tulsi is a practicing Hindu, I'm a practicing Muslim, and while for many people that would be seen as a difference, we only saw our common motivation to serve God. Life poses many difficult challenges, and when those moments come, both of us turn to prayer, scripture, and spiritual guides. That shared commitment allowed me and Tulsi immediately to cut through all the superficial bullshit and build a real relationship.

———

I couldn't help myself as that first conversation turned into a game plan. It was pretty clear to me off the bat that Tulsi was not associating herself with the right people. She had to rush off for a dinner, but she was in town for a few days and we met a couple more times. Later on she came through San Francisco and asked if I would put her through a workout. I said yes, so she came into Empower. When we got started, she said, "Don't take it easy on me." That, of course, was totally unnecessary. I never take it easy on anyone. She was surprised at how simple I kept everything as we did some elementary body weight exercises. As she went through the movements I whispered to her about the importance of breathing and embracing the discomfort she was feeling. "Don't hold back," I said. "Let yourself overcome it." After about twenty minutes she was done.

We sat on the floor for a while afterward and talked. It was a very emotional conversation. That's what happens when you introduce the physical component to the game plan.

Tulsi and I continued to have regular conversations on the phone and over FaceTime. As her presidential run was winding down, I could hear the hurt in her voice. I probed into this feeling, and eventually she recognized that it stemmed from those moments she was doing her best to break through the political noise and communicate to the American people why she was offering to serve them, only to be met by obstacles and attempts to silence her by mainstream politicians and media.

What I discovered through these sessions was that Tulsi has a very optimistic view of people. I would go so far as to say that she is naïve, but in a good way in that she sees the best in people. Her intention to serve is real, but she is sometimes surprised when others don't operate in the same way.

The fact is, there are very few people who operate like her. Just look at her military record. How can you not respect that? Nobody drafted Tulsi into the service. She enlisted and volunteered to deploy to Iraq during the height of the war. In this way, Tulsi reminds me a lot of my mom—which is the highest compliment I can pay any person, male or female. She fought through all those hardships so she could give her family a better life. My mom was never about herself and always about serving others. Tulsi is the same way.

Tulsi has seen in both politics and the military how paralyzing fear can be. In the U.S. Capitol, she is surrounded by fellow legislators who live in fear—of not getting reelected, of people not liking them, of feeling like they're on the fringes of their social circles. It's kind of like being back in high school again. This is especially problematic because that pervasive fear doesn't just hurt those individuals, it also hurts the country. If you're making decisions out of self-preservation as opposed to for the public good, it severely reduces your impact. Tulsi's challenge was to avoid falling into that trap.

———

After Tulsi dropped out of the presidential race in the midst of the COVID pandemic, she shared with me how frustrated she was with the way people on Capitol Hill and in the media had treated her candidacy. When I heard her speak of this, I closed my eyes and prayed that God would give me something that I could pass along to her to make sense of her pain. I reached an important insight: the reason she was thinking this way was that she believed it was all her fault, that if only she had done more, and done things differently, maybe there would have been a different result.

This is a common dynamic with a lot of people I'm blessed to coach and work with. So many of their frustrations with society are really frustrations with themselves. The natural piece of advice in these situations is "Work on yourself," but why do we have to consider it work? Just do it. Forgive yourself. Do you love you? Do you trust the intentions you have and why you want to feel a certain way? You can give this gift to yourself, so why not choose to do it? Why do you want to make it so difficult to give yourself what you know you need in order to have peace? How much time are you going to waste?

I emphasized to Tulsi that she had one great asset in this situation: she is a young woman. Before her fortieth birthday, Tulsi had served two tours in the military, spent eight years in the U.S. Congress, and made a high-profile run for president. That's a pretty good start. "God loves you," I said. "You have a long and beautiful life ahead, with so much opportunity to serve, grow and learn about yourself. You can evolve a lot—and you will."

As a member of Congress, some would say that Tulsi has been very hard to pin down ideologically. She has her share of both supporters and critics on the far left and the far right. Through our conversations, I try to help Tulsi think even more outside the box. I never ask her what she wants. I ask what impact she wants to have. Then we work our way backward, forward, inside, outside—every which way we can.

I'm helping her network in the worlds that I inhabit, from sports to business to entertainment to entrepreneurship. My message to her is the same as my message to you: Let's work to conquer the disease of fear. For everyone, the central question is different. In Tulsi's case, it's always about how she can best serve God and seize the opportunity He has given her to surrender to Him and put everything in His hands. If she can do that, she is liberated from fear.

I take my guidance on this from the Quran. This life is temporary. What's one moment of rejection when measured against that? So why not battle and compete? Why not experience things?

Our desire to play it safe keeps us stuck in the same old routines. We're focused on what we might lose, and as a result we lose out on so many potential gains.

Tulsi may be a politician, but she has never viewed politics as a career. She is constantly asking herself how she can best serve God and His children. I have full respect for the office of the presidency, but I'm not overly enamored of politicians. There is a bigger picture at play.

<hr>

Another thing that Tulsi and I share is a commitment to normalize the narrative around mental health. She saw firsthand in the military how admitting a mental health challenge is equated with weakness. It's similar to what I've seen in sports. Young, strong men and women who carry guns are not supposed to admit they're sad or anxious. They're supposed to "tough it out." They don't realize that their inability to "admit weakness" is itself a weakness. This goes for whether they are in combat or dealing with issues like PTSD once they get back home.

Tulsi has a unique perspective on this because she has been a private, an enlisted soldier, and she has also been a platoon leader, a company commander, and currently serves as a lieutenant colonel. She has been led by great leaders and also by commanders who were trying to exude strength but really ended up being weak because they were putting up a façade. When it was her turn to lead, Tulsi found ways to express her "weaknesses" as a person and a leader. If she made mistakes, she admitted them and promised to learn from them. Rather than causing her unit to lose faith,

Tulsi realized that her openness and transparency established trust. Her recognition of her "weaknesses" did not make her weak at all. It strengthened her and therefore enabled her to make a greater impact.

This is why I have made it a priority at this stage of my life to bring my philosophies to the military. I am working with a team of data scientists to bring this ideology to the military to help combat suicide, post-traumatic stress disorder, schizophrenia, and heart disease. I firmly believe that once people understand that admitting they suffer from these problems is not a sign of weakness, then they will find they have extraordinary strength to make their lives better.

Is Tulsi misunderstood? I wouldn't put it quite like that. I'd say she has yet to fully articulate to the world who she really is. That's going to take some time and intentional choices on her part. It's also going to require some better judgments about who she is surrounding herself with. It's the same set of questions I would ask of anyone. Do these people next to you really share your values? Do they share your goals? Your intense desire to serve? If the answer is no, can you see why that would make you feel boxed in? If you do, then it's time to get out of the box.

Once Tulsi left Congress in January 2021, the shackles came off. She is still a big-time surfer. Almost every morning when she's at home, she's out in the ocean catching waves. I still think she has a future in politics, which I hope includes another run for president. In the meantime, she is free to go out and integrate her perspective and philosophy with organizations around the world. She will be able to start new initiatives that place her finger on the trigger of her own destiny. As much as she has already accomplished at such a young age, Tulsi remains motivated by her faith in God, always looking to serve and evolve. She has achieved a great deal, and yet her days of maximum impact are still ahead of her.

CHAPTER FIVE

PERMISSION

Every single one of us has the ability to choose how we want to feel, yet we restrict ourselves out of fear. We know how we want to feel, but we don't give ourselves permission. I catch myself doing this all the time. This leads me to accept someone else's way of thinking instead of trusting my own gut. It's just human nature. Giving yourself permission can be scary, so we don't do it. It's easier to blame someone else when things don't work out.

I have noticed this when I work with high achievers. I use that phrase because that's what they are considered in the eyes of "normal" society, but for that very reason they are more susceptible to falling into the permission trap. They get fanboyed all the time, as they are surrounded by people who ooh and aah at how brilliant they are. I've worked with many millionaires who have forgotten how to earn things. They have the resources to build a certain feeling, but they don't use them.

This is what permission is all about. We need to give ourselves permission to feel pain. Truly successful people—by my definition—put themselves in the position to experience pain because they realize that is the only path that leads to the best version of themselves. They choose professions that force them to stay on their toes. They don't want to be surrounded by fanboys. They want to trust their guts, take risks, and bring others along.

This is my challenge to you: Give yourself permission to trust your gut. If you do that, there is nothing to fear. Whatever happens is true to your experience.

The responsibility that comes along with this permission can be scary, but you can deal with it as long as you are aware of what is happening. My primary intention with this book is to normalize the narratives around mental health. I want you to stop avoiding what society has told you isn't "normal." Stop putting glass ceilings over your head. Trust yourself. Take the risk.

This is not something you can turn on like a light switch. This is a behavioral practice. If you train for a marathon and run the race, you're not going to train for the next marathon exactly the same way. Each challenge is different, so each process to prepare is different. If you give yourself permission to get lost in the process, you'll be okay with being afraid of the potential outcomes. Marshawn Lynch doesn't win every football game, and Jake Shields doesn't win every fight. They don't prepare for each battle the same way. They do it better each time.

Same with faith. If you want to be true to your faith, you have to practice the behaviors and principles. In Islam, we pray five times a day. There's a ritual that goes along with that, and certain guidelines: Wash your body, abstain from alcohol, don't steal.

You're supposed to be as clean as possible when you step onto a prayer rug. If you just do that once, you are not practicing your faith. But if you are truly committed, you do it over and over again. This requires a willingness to accept responsibility. You can't take that first step unless you give yourself permission.

What's interesting about a spiritual practice is that the more you become aware of it, the more anxiety you will feel. People assume that practicing faith makes anxiety go away, but what it actually does is *normalize* that anxiety. Believe me, there are times when I wish I were more aloof and didn't feel this deep awareness. With awareness comes responsibility, and with responsibility comes angst. You can't have one without the other, and you shouldn't *want* to have one without the other. That's what the power of permission can do for you.

Sadly, I believe our society has been depriving itself of this permission. I saw how people struggled during the Covid-19 pandemic, but I saw other people adapt very quickly and find the blessings they needed to carry on, even after losing their jobs. The whole situation forced people to believe in something other than humankind, because for the first time our generation had to confront something that was infinitesimally small and yet much bigger than we are. We had to relearn a lot about humility, kindness, and community. The virus forced us into the very spaces we were refusing to give ourselves permission to enter.

My hope is that as a result of that difficult experience, people will give themselves permission to achieve this understanding without relying on others to tell us how to feel. Give yourself permission to be independent with your feelings. Your feelings are what expose your thoughts, and your thoughts expose your actions. Everybody on this planet has the opportunity and the ability to serve in some capacity, but we rob ourselves of that experience because of a false narrative. Go ahead and do it. Give yourself permission to be independent. It's a critical tool in conquering the disease of fear.

As I entered my senior year at Fresno State, I thought I knew very clearly the path ahead. I had it all planned out. I knew it wouldn't be easy, but I could see the challenges and understood how I wanted to overcome them. I had no idea how wrong I was, but that's how it is with plans. In order to adapt to the changing reality, I had to give myself that permission to trust my gut and accept the fear I was feeling. That permission led me to a very scary place, but it was the only place on the planet where I could truly begin to fulfill my purpose.

———

I worked my ass off to be in the best shape of my life for my senior season. Things took off after my head coach Pat Hill pulled me aside and told me I could have a successful future at fullback. I was instantly sold. That's the one position on the field where you're asked to do everything—run, block, and catch. I got a new jersey number but kept my locker next to my boys on defense.

Meanwhile, my close buddy Dave Tollefson was having a tough time. We came to Fresno State together, but prior to leaving junior college Dave tore his labrum, and his season ended up being really disrupted by injuries. After yet another shoulder surgery in 2001, he left school to work as a carpenter. He basically gave up on football.

He came back to Fresno State to catch a couple of my games. I remember running up the ramp at halftime and hearing him call my name. I looked into the stands and saw that Dave was crying. It meant so much to him to see me playing Division I football for a highly ranked program after all I had been through. He was so moved by that that he decided to give football one more try. He enrolled at Northwest Missouri State, which has one of the top Division II programs in the country. He got healthy, became a Division II All-American at defensive end and linebacker, was selected by the Green Bay Packers in the seventh round of the 2006 draft, and eventually won two Super Bowls with the New York Giants.

My experience in football helped keep my mind off the stress in my family. During my senior year, my father went back to Afghanistan to try to settle the land disputes he was having. I knew what he was trying to do was important, but I was fixated on my goal of making the NFL. The better I played, the more I thought about a career after college. I saw players I had gone up against getting shots at the NFL, and I felt I was just as good if not better than they were. Realistically, I didn't think my game performances would be good enough to get me drafted, but I knew that a lot of players used a "pro day" as a springboard to the league. That's where a bunch of NFL scouts and executives come to campus and watch graduating players work out, kind of like a private pre-draft combine. I had heard stories of guys who didn't necessarily have great careers do well on their forty-yard dashes and bench-press sets and end up getting drafted. I decided that would be my best path.

Preparing for my pro day became my main focus throughout the season. I had a great base of knowledge of training, from not just football but my boxing and martial arts past, and no one was more determined. I knew the odds were long, but I was going to give it my very best shot.

Unfortunately, my body broke down on me. It started with this really weird pain in my left glute. The only time I felt better was when I was lying down. I had to pop a dozen Alleves just to get through the day. The pain moved to my back, but I didn't want that to stop me, either. That is, until the week of our battle against Colorado State, when I was running the ball at practice and took a nasty hit. I felt a terrific jolt go through my back and tingling in my leg.

Finally, I went to the trainer, who sent me to a neurologist. He gave me an epidural injection, which worked for a few days, but the pain flared up on me again. This time, the neurologist gave me an MRI, and it showed I had two herniated discs. I played through the pain the rest of the season, but by the time we were playing Michigan State in the Silicon Valley Bowl, I could barely walk. I didn't even dress for that game.

I had to give in and agree to surgery, which I had in early January. Needless to say, this hampered my preparations for my pro day. At that point, I was in so much pain I didn't even care so much about football. I just wanted to be able to walk. The surgeon performed a microdiscectomy, and I thought I was healing quickly. Of course, I tried to come back too soon. I remember doing some simple medicine ball stuff and feeling a sharp pain where the stitches were. It was the start of a staph infection, which can be life-threatening if it gets into your spine. They shot me up with antibiotics and I was popping Vicodin like candy. The whole thing really wore me down. I felt myself becoming this super-negative person, and I also could sense a problem with pills coming on. So I stopped taking them.

By the end of my senior year, I had to face a difficult reality: my pro day was not going to happen, which almost certainly meant I would never play in the NFL. That was a bitter pill to swallow, but it also forced me to take my life in a dramatically different direction. I had been thinking of making the change anyway, but I wasn't giving myself permission to fulfill my destiny. That was about to change.

———

By the time my father knew what I was doing, I was already in Dubai. I called him from the airport and told him I was on my way to Afghanistan. He was shocked. He tried to talk me out of coming, but I wouldn't hear of it. The next day, I landed in Kabul, my first time setting foot in the country that I had heard so much about all my life.

I made the surprise trip because I couldn't stand hearing about all the ways my father was being screwed by his own family. I wasn't getting great information, and I was truly worried about him. My dad was kind and nonconfrontational. It was easy to take advantage of him. I wanted to confront the assholes who were stealing his family name and assets. They didn't know it yet, but that quiet man had raised a lion, and they were about to meet him face-to-face.

Arriving in Afghanistan was an emotional experience. I started choking up while I was still on the runway. As I was walking off the plane, my father was waiting for me on the runway at the bottom of the stairs. He looked so frail. The whole ordeal was taking a massive toll on him. He had come to meet me along with a couple of local warlords who were helping him try to resolve all these family disputes. He hugged me and said, "It's okay, you're safe here."

I was not in a good frame of mind. While I was on that plane I was getting very angry and frustrated with the people around me. A lot of people in Afghanistan lack basic etiquette and hygiene. There is no education. People have no manners. Many passengers on that flight had bare feet, they were spitting tobacco on the floor, picking their noses, and starting all kinds of problems. I reminded myself that I was privileged to have been a refugee and given opportunities they weren't. I wondered how we could have any expectations for a country filled with people like this.

When I left for Afghanistan, I had nasty intentions. I wanted to go there and do whatever it took to protect my father's legacy and his name. If they were going to try to kill me, I would have to kill them first. I was primed and ready to do anything to stand up for my family. You can talk about killing people when you're in America, but in Afghanistan it's like drinking water. It's nothing to those people. I prepared myself mentally to join the fight.

I wasn't in the country more than a few hours before my mindset started to change. More than that—I felt deeply ashamed. I took a deep breath and saw the beautiful mountains of Kabul, and I became overcome with emotion. I knew that I had more to give to this place than more pain and blood. How could I possibly come here and add to the bloodbath? What kind of human being was I, especially after I had been lucky enough to get out of there and be raised in America, where I played sports, made friends, and got an education?

I decided my purpose in the world would be to disrupt the country of Afghanistan and make things better by drawing on my knowledge, experience, and resources. I gave myself full permission to pursue this mission. I believed I was going to make things better. I just didn't know how.

———

We drove from the airport to our family's house on Chicken Street. If you know anything about Afghan history and culture, then you know about Chicken Street. During the 1970s, it was a big tourist attraction, with all kinds of shops to see and things to do. I had always heard about how vibrant the street was and how wonderful the home was that we had there.

What I found, however, was a much different story. Our house was in horrible shape. The walls were full of bullet holes. There were no screens on the windows, no furniture anywhere. There were a couple of mattresses on the floor, and that was it. Here I thought I was coming to a palace, and instead I found this shithole. What did I get myself into?

There was, however, an early glimmer of hope. When I got to the house, tons of neighborhood kids swarmed me. They had heard I was a football player from America, but they thought I played *futbol*, meaning soccer. I laughed and told them they were wrong, but it didn't matter, because pretty soon we were playing a pickup soccer game right there in the neighborhood. Before long kids came from all over to join the game. I loved the joy and the free-spirited way the kids played. It reminded me of my cousins in San Francisco. It was like getting hit with a bolt of spiritual lightning. I had learned firsthand when I was growing up the power that sports had to bring people together. I knew at that moment that if I could bring that power to Afghanistan, it would create the disruption I was seeking.

Now that I was on the ground, I had to figure out the rules of engagement. All these people who called themselves friends of my father came to the house and kissed my ass, but I knew I couldn't trust any of them. After all, many of them were the same people who had gone behind my father's back and screwed him out of his inheritance. As you can probably guess, I have never been the quiet type, but that's the persona I had to adopt at the beginning. I spent a lot of time sitting, listening, analyzing, and figuring out my next move. I knew how important this was to my dad. There was no way I was going to let him fail.

A lot of locals were engaging me and trying to get me into their camps. Many of them had small militias working for them. It was very overwhelming and confusing. And yet, my dad treated everyone so well. After a couple of weeks I said to him, "How can you not see what pieces of shit these people are?" He tried to calm me by saying he was playing a long game.

I would never have gotten through those first few months in Afghanistan without the help of Malik Zarine. He was a very influential person in the eastern region of Afghanistan. He was considered one of the most notorious gangsters, and of course I didn't agree with many of the ways in which he operated. But I had to consider that I was not in America anymore. The rules were different here. This was the way things went.

I first met Malik through my father when they picked me up at the airport in Kabul. Malik and I quickly built a close relationship. He was very excited that I had been raised in America but was so passionate about my family legacy. The fact that I was willing to sacrifice my life of comfort to serve my father gave me a lot of street cred in that country. Over time, it made me feel confident enough to take chances to get things done.

You have to understand that while in America we refer to certain people as gangsters and warlords, in Afghanistan they are considered tribal leaders. They're the ones who are doing something for the people. Violence is a way of life over there, so the only way to get things done is to project strength. This hit me right away—like *Holy shit, I am working with some* real *gangsters now.* I had to learn to be bold and cautious at the same time.

The more I saw my father having these conversations with people I knew were screwing him, the more pessimistic I became. I was glad to know that Malik Zarine and his militia were giving us their support. On my father's recommendation, I called my uncle Ehsan. A lot of big decisions in my life went through him. I told my uncle that all these guys were coming to our house and spinning all this bullshit to my dad, and he was believing all of it. I started to figure out that some of my father's siblings had sold some property even though they didn't own the deeds. What was my dad's response to that? "They are poor. They don't have the life we have in America."

I knew I couldn't leave the country until all of this was figured out. I didn't care how long it took. I got used to seeing arguments that led people to draw their guns. The first time someone pulled one on me, it felt like a dream. But I had dealt with some bad boys in the Bay Area and in college, and I learned early on that a lot of these guys talk shit, but as soon as you get in their face they back down. I got a couple of AK-47s and a 9mm Makarov handgun to protect myself. I also recovered my grandfather's gun that had been given to him by the president of Turkey. It was a small handgun that could fit in my palm.

I kept up the strong, silent act for several weeks. Then one day we were sitting in the living room and my father was talking about what he wanted to do moving forward with his farmland, mines, and other real estate. His brother-in-law kept interrupting him and trying to overrule my father, saying, "Oh, well, that is not what we are going to do." Finally my dad looked over at me and nodded. He was finally ready to turn his lion loose.

All those weeks of listening and burning inside exploded right out of me. I jumped up and got right in this guy's face. I pulled out my 9mm revolver so he could see it. Of course, he had no idea there were no bullets in it. I told him in no uncertain terms that if he ever disrespected my father like that again there would be a very heavy price to pay. "When my father speaks," I told him, "you put your head down and listen."

I turned on the other men in the room and went nuts on them. "You all have been taking advantage of my father for too long," I said. "You know why he's been so quiet about all of this for twenty years? Because he has been raising me. So everything he wants now he's going to get, because I'm here to make sure he gets it. And if you try to stop him, I will make sure you regret it."

I could say I don't know what got into me, but actually I do. Afghanistan got into me. That's what the place does. There was no water, no electricity, my body was dirty, my clothes were dirty. I was losing it, man. But once word got around about what I had done, the locals respected me. They knew I was serious about protecting my family, and I didn't need anyone else's permission to do it.

The Game Plan: Jed York Gives Himself Permission

One night I was watching television and saw yet another unflattering story about Jed York, the CEO of the San Francisco 49ers. The Niners were a shit show at that point, and Jed was taking most of the heat. There were airplanes flying banners over their home games calling for Jed to sell the team. Living in San Francisco, I'd seen a bunch of these stories, and each one pissed me off tremendously. The guy I was seeing on my TV was not the Jed I knew. He is a really smart man, but there was obviously something preventing him from operating at full capacity. He was going up against a glass ceiling, and for whatever reason he wasn't giving himself permission to break through.

I grabbed my phone and sent Jed a text letting him know that I was thinking about him. I told him it was time for us to get to work. He replied immediately. We agreed to meet at Empower the following Monday.

I had first met Jed at a coffee shop in Palo Alto a year before. We got connected through mutual friends who were concerned about him and the direction the team was heading. Jed and I immediately made profound connections. Like me, he had inherited a very heavy family legacy. His grandfather was Ed DeBartolo Sr., who built up a hugely successful construction business and bought the 49ers in 1977. DeBartolo's daughter, Denise York, is Jed's mother, and she is the current owner and cochair of the team. Jed grew up in Youngstown, Ohio, where he was captain of his high school baseball team. He played baseball for Notre Dame, and soon after graduating he started working for the 49ers. He was all of twenty-eight years old when his mother appointed him team president.

Yeah, yeah, I know, no one wants to play violins for a dude who was born into a family of billionaires, but as my family history indicates, that can be a major burden, and Jed was really feeling it. Between 2011 and 2013, the team had gone to three NFC Championship games and a Super Bowl, but the next season things got nasty between Jed and the head coach, Jim Harbaugh, and it got played out in the press. Jed fired him after the Niners went 8-8 in 2014. The next two coaches each lasted just one season each, with Chip Kelly going 2-14 in 2016. Kelly's replacement, Kyle Shanahan, won six games his first season. The fans were pissed and Jed was feeling discouraged.

Jed struck me as one of those guys who are honest to a fault, just like Marshawn Lynch—and me, for that matter. He could be a little rough with reporters, but I knew from my own experience that when you have a purpose in life, you have to be willing to prove it at all costs.

Jed and I both had grandfathers who showed us it's okay not

to be "normal." He was willing to be the face of the family business, which is not easy at such a young age. Yeah, he's got this huge inheritance, but he's not interested in sitting at home and collecting checks. He cares deeply about his legacy.

Just like my father, Jed had to deal with this challenge knowing there were people close to him who were trying to undermine him. Not only is that bad for business, but it can really sap a leader's confidence.

When Jed and I met at the coffee shop, I shared some of the details of my own family history. There are not many people who can understand that part of me like he did. Statistics show that most family businesses sharply decline or go under by the third generation. Jed was very aware of this, so he was on edge in an effort to stave off that erosion. That's why he found my personal story so haunting. My family history shows how quickly things can change. Just because someone is born on top of a pile of cash doesn't mean it will still be there by the time his children become adults.

You might think it was a steeper challenge for me to enter Jed's life during this low point. I thought it was a great privilege. It forced us to engage on a deep level from the start. As you can tell by now, I am not fond of chitchat.

And yet, Jed was a little skeptical at first. He wondered if I was for real. He was used to so many people trying to BS him in hopes of squeezing some money out of him. Was I just another grifter? Or did I really mean what I was saying? He was also used to getting pitches from trainers and performance coaches with grand promises about transforming his players into winners. Imagine his shock when I said I had zero interest in doing any sort of business with his players, or his team for that matter. My interest was in him.

We bumped fists and promised to keep our friendship active. In the months that followed, we texted and called and saw each other occasionally, but we never committed to pursuing something deeper. That changed the night I saw that story on TV. I knew in my bones that Jed had all kinds of potential, but he wasn't ready to give himself full permission to reach it. I decided that needed to change.

———

The morning after our text exchange, Jed arrived at Empower dressed to work out. He is a former college baseball player and still plays a lot of basketball, so he has kept himself in good physical form. I kind of smirked as I led him to my office so we could do a game plan. I assured him we would have a workout, but first I wanted to talk. He gave me that quizzical look I've seen so many times, and then he took a seat.

I went straight for the jugular. "My job here is to focus on restricted potential," I said. "I want to know what's preventing you from being the Jed I know you are. I know you're doing this for a bigger reason than most people think. Yeah, getting to a Super Bowl is awesome, but you are playing for something much bigger here. I want to know why you're not giving yourself permission to achieve it."

I shared more details of my life. In doing so, I let him know this was a space where we could keep it real and talk about what was really going on—what we were really afraid of. He felt a debt to his grandfather because he went against all odds and found a way to win. That led to a bigger discussion about what was happening within the 49ers organization. It became apparent that he was holding himself back, that he was not doing what was best for himself and the franchise because he was trying to please so many people. Losing brings out losers, and because of the team's struggles, and because of the messy way in which Harbaugh left as head coach, a lot of snipers and backstabbers were taking their shots. Jed got pounded, but the hardest part was he didn't know who was for him and who was against him. That was the price he was paying for not being true to himself and running things the way he really wanted to.

During our game plan, I could see that Jed was feeling very alone. That's hard for someone like him because he is trained not to show vulnerability. Jed got emotional as he shared his frustrations. He couldn't get others to see his higher purpose. And all the negative publicity was hurting his family.

Finally we did our first workout. I'm used to dealing with people who are fit. I always go after what has been neglected. I've done this long enough now that it feels like a gift. It's a cool way for me to lower the waterline and get them relaxed about being vulnerable. It's not about spotting weakness, it's about evaluating capacity. You're never strong enough and you're never too weak. There's always room to optimize. I try to get people to adopt that mind-set because it correlates to life. Too often, we allow ourselves to settle for what we are. We stay comfortable. My job is to disrupt that.

I love seeing the looks on people's faces when we start the physical portion of our work. They're expecting all this fancy equipment and cute gimmicks that other trainers use. Then I come along and ask them to do some simple push-ups. We move to basic body weight movements. Wherever you're weaker in your body, that's what I focus on. Throughout the workout we conduct a running conversation about family, goals, and dreams. It's a lot easier to have those talks when a person's guard is down. The things that come out are real.

I typically get into a routine with a teammate for two or three months, and then I change it around so they're not just using the same muscles over and over again. The actions I teach work especially well for people like Jed who travel a lot. Contrary to what most people think, you don't need a fancy hotel gym to get in a good workout. You just need a little bit of space and a strong attitude. That also goes for eating, which is a huge challenge for the business traveler.

Jed has always tried to keep himself on an even keel. He learned the hard way that you're never as good as what people say about you when you're on top, and you're never as bad as what they say when you're down. This became more challenging when he got married in 2011 and had kids. Having a family made Jed a lot more sensitive to outside criticism, because he knew his wife would hear what people were saying. Part of my mission was to help him understand that he could be a champion in the business world without sacrificing stability at home. He also wanted to make sure that his inheritance didn't become a burden on his own children. He wants them to find peace as they look to extend the family legacy, which makes it doubly important for him to set the right example.

Beginning with that first meeting, Jed and I worked on giving himself permission to build a new narrative, not as an inheritor of the DeBartolo legacy but as a man who could build something everlasting. Jed needed to know that a legacy is not built alone. He had to become involved with people who were philosophically aligned. Think about the people in your life. How many of them will be there at the morgue to wash your body? Those are the ones who are real. It's up to us to build relationships with them.

That was going to be the crux of Jed's new narrative. He had to reorient his life and his business around those people and those relationships. He needed to prioritize facts over feelings. If someone is going to be a cancer in an organization, it doesn't matter how you feel about him—he has to go. Jed had to make strong decisions about the personalities he wanted to build his legacy around. At the end of the day, that space is his house, and he needed to give himself permission to hold that line and make sure everyone knew where he stood.

———

As often happens with my teammate, Jed and I got extremely close. You can't share the things we shared without feeling like you're family.

One day Jed called to ask if I would meet with his young brother, Tony, who was dealing with heavy emotional and mental challenges. Even worse, he was in a deep state of denial about what was happening. Of course I said yes. Tony grew up wrestling and was really into martial arts and MMA. We had some troubling moments where he described things that were not really happening. I'm not a medical professional, so I don't want to diagnose what was going on with Tony, but clearly there were some chemical imbalances at issue. I don't believe he was ever able to get to a point where he could understand and process that.

Tragically, things got to the point where Tony decided to take his own life. Jed called me the night he went missing, and I was with him when he learned the news. It was painful to watch him and his family go through that. I knew what it was like to deal with mental illness in the family, so I know it could have easily been someone close to me who died by suicide. Of course, there was nothing Jed could have done—he had been an amazing brother to Tony—but it is natural to feel survivor's guilt. I would feel the same way if my kid brother died.

I never did a straight-up game plan with Tony. He would only let me in so far. In some ways he was too smart for his own good. He was able to hide a lot of what was really going on inside his head and his emotions. If I started to get too close, he pulled away. He was never able to let down his guard with me and speak about what was causing his instability and his fears. I have lost a few friends to suicide, and so I know how painful the experience can be. I can help someone do this kind of work, but I can't do it for him. He has to be a willing participant. Tony is on my mind every day, and I pray for his spirit every morning in my Fajr prayers.

Jed knows how close I am with my younger brother, Yossef. Watching him and his family go through that ordeal provided us with another connection. For Jed, dealing with Tony's suicide has

been a process. It's not like one day you just let it go. I know he
thinks about his brother every day. It has given Jed a deeper understanding of the people who matter in his life.

————

When Jed I first started working together at Empower, he would
come to downtown San Francisco a couple of times per week.
That's a long way for him, so instead of him having to make the
drive to Empower each week, Jed asked me what it would look like
if we brought Empower directly to the 49ers. I was super flattered
and ready to deliver, because I knew I could bring my concepts to
the organization to achieve the results he desired. Again, I wasn't
interested in working with his players but rather his sales, operation, and executive teams. My feeling was that unless there was a
championship culture throughout the organization, they would
never have one on the field. I wanted to help him build it.

Jed gave us a good-sized space to create Empower at the team's
complex in Santa Clara. My staff and I put Jed's employees through
the paces. Those sessions helped bring Jed's people together, which
in turn enabled them to stay true to their collective mission. I love
seeing these executives working hard and breathing heavy in the
middle of their workday. There's a special connection people have
when they are in that environment. In the office, you're always
trying to show off what you know and what you can accomplish.
In a workout, you're exposing your vulnerability.

Although I train a lot of NFL players, I have never been interested in working with teams, because my presence can be considered a threat. But after a year with the 49ers' executives, I started

sharing with Jed my vision for an in-house player performance department. Having been around the NFL about a decade, I came to believe that teams were making a mistake by not having performance directors who were a permanent part of the team's infrastructure. Instead, most times the head coaches set up their strength programs. There are two problems with this. First, oftentimes those coaches hire their friends as opposed to the best people for the job. Sometimes they'll move a position coach into the performance role, as if those skill sets are the same. Second, head coaches come and go, but the organization stays the same. That interrupts continuity and robs the franchise of data that has been collected on its players. I've also seen how a lot of big corporations do business, and I thought NFL teams needed more of that mindset. I strongly believed that the strength and performance operation should belong to the team, and then integrated with the coaches when they enter the franchise.

When I first presented my idea to Jed, he pushed back pretty hard. It's not that he's opposed to new ideas, he just wants to test the conviction and reasoning of the person presenting it. Over time, Jed ran the idea by members of his own team and they agreed this was the right move. I was tempted to make a push to take on this position myself, but it didn't make sense because I had so many things going on with my business. So instead I worked closely with their process to find a leader for their performance department, and then supported the leadership any way I could.

The reason this performance operation is so effective isn't that the ideas are so earth-shattering. It's that it provides across-the-board coordination that pulls everything together, from the strength team to the medical team to the physical therapists to mental health staff. This is not innovation, it's common sense, yet I don't know of any other NFL team that operates this way.

I believe the concept of performance is transferable and scalable. Whether it's a tech company, a hedge fund, an auto repair shop, or a police department, every organization should have a person or department that is devoted to optimizing people's performance capacities. What's a higher priority than how your workers perform?

Why is this so important? Because performance is where the truth lives. Those workouts are the only place where people show vulnerability. It's the only place they cry. There's no hiding in the performance department. Think about the training room for a sports team. You don't just have trainers in there taping ankles. There's a physical therapist, a nutritionist, sometimes even a psychotherapist. It's where athletes can come and know they will be safe from judgment.

I think Jed is at a good place in his life now. He is much more in touch with his mental and emotional states, and he's gotten much better at managing disappointments—better than me, anyway. That was apparent after the 49ers lost to the Kansas City Chiefs in Super Bowl LIV. I'll be honest, I don't do well with losses. Remember, on top of my relationship with the club I was raised a Niners fan. I pout when they lose a regular season game, much less the Super Bowl.

After the game was over, Jed and I rode with a group of people from the stadium back to the event hall where a big reception was taking place for the team. I didn't want to socialize, though. I wanted to sulk. So I went back to my hotel room. Thirty minutes later, I got a text from Jed asking where I was. When I told him I was in my room, he asked me to come back to the party. His team had just lost the Super Bowl, yet he was the one who wanted to lift my spirits.

After all Jed had been through, he was very upbeat and positive that night. He knew his organization had come a long way under his leadership and that it would learn all the right lessons from the loss. He had given himself permission to reach his potential, and he was seeing benefits that went well beyond reaching the Super Bowl. He didn't just break through that glass ceiling, he shattered it into a million tiny pieces. It made me feel so honored to be not just his teammate but his brother.

CHAPTER SIX

SELFLESSNESS

When I first got to Afghanistan, I had no idea how long I was going to stay. Month after month passed, and I was still there. To help pay the bills and buy groceries, I worked all kinds of side hustles. I would come back to the States for a few weeks to train my fighters and make some cash. Then I would go back to Afghanistan and figure out how to make ends meet. When you grow up the way I did, you either learn to be resourceful or you don't eat.

Over time, I was able to help my father recover a lot of his land and get it back in our family's name. But dealing with all these scumbags and trying to play the intimidation game took a toll on me. I found myself looking for outlets where I could inflict positive change as well.

This was the essence of my Afghanistan education. I went there for the most selfish of reasons. First, I wanted to slap all those evil double-crossers who were screwing over the person I loved more than any other in the world. I was determined to uphold the integrity of our land and not let these crooks benefit from my father's life work. I was evolving as a businessman and starting to make a little bit of money. Those are not bad things, by the way. They were all necessary. But they weren't enough.

Over time, my selfishness gave way to self*less*ness. I don't believe this is a natural human progression. I loved my father very much, but his lack of selfishness was a very real flaw. It kept him from living his truth, which in turn prevented him from helping out his family and the country he so desperately wanted to serve. He was generous in his heart, but too often he denied himself the tools to translate that feeling into action.

That was not the case with me, his lion. I had strong muscles and big-ass teeth, and now my selfless instincts drove me to want to take a bite out of my country and make a real difference. But how?

My mind kept returning to that impromptu soccer game I had played with the neighborhood kids upon my arrival. It was a vivid demonstration of the power of sports to unite people and spur change. So I dove in and helped the soccer federation open programs for kids all over the country. I had seen this happening in the example of Shamila Kohestani. She had shown promise as a young soccer player in Afghanistan, so much so that in 2004 she was sent to the United States to participate in a clinic hosted by the Afghan Youth Sports Exchange, a nonprofit organization. She returned to the States two years later to attend the Julie Foudy Soccer Leadership Academy in New Jersey and then got her degree at Drew University in Madison, New Jersey.

Anwar Jekdelek, who was the president of the Olympic Federation, understood and supported my vision to use sports to help forge peace throughout the region. Anwar was a former Olympic wrestler, and we bonded over our mutual cauliflower ears. I was amazed at how few of the members of the federation had actually played sports. I showed them how to develop neighborhood soccer programs like the ones I had played in back home.

In 2006, Shamila was among a group of girls, which also included Roya Zaka, who were given the prestigious Arthur Ashe Award Courage Award at the ESPYs in Los Angeles for their role in using sports to spark a women's movement inside Afghanistan. She and Roya accepted the award before a TV audience of millions. They were the faces of hope for social advancement in a country that had been so badly war-torn for decades.

As a member of the coaching staff, I was invited to attend the ESPYs with Shamila and the girls to watch them receive the award. I met several well-known athletes and TV personalities and was able to share my experiences in Afghanistan with them. It was a beautiful night, but I also saw how these women could be used as PR props to paint a picture that wasn't completely true and that mostly served the desires of leaders in Afghanistan who didn't have the best intentions. Shamila, in fact, was later excommunicated from the soccer program in Afghanistan and has spent the ensuing years traveling the world to speak on behalf of the power of sports to make meaningful social change.

One year later, Afghanistan formed its very first women's national soccer team. They played most of their home games in Ghazi National Olympic Stadium in Kabul, but they also traveled to places like Pakistan, Germany, and Jordan to train and compete.

They would go on to compete in the South Asian Football Federation and the South Asian Games.

By this time I was starting to make a name for myself. People were gravitating to the disruptive new *futbol* coach from America who was supporting local head coaches like the legendary Wali Saboorzada. They sensed my selfless instincts and trusted that I was genuinely trying to help my country recover from all the devastation. But I was also working on selfish motives because I very much needed to be accepted as someone who could add value to this cause. People would thank and praise me, but I would tell them, "This is more for me than it is for you." They thought I was joking.

A big thing working in my favor was the fact that my mom would never let me do business with government contractors. That meant turning down some lucrative opportunities, but it allowed me to avoid working with people who had different intentions. They didn't care about Afghanistan, they just wanted to satisfy their own greed. It entrenched my reputation for selflessness even further. It made the locals more likely to trust and help me. Like my mom always said, in our family, we don't take bricks, we lay bricks.

———

As time went on and my confidence grew, I let my mind go to impossible places. I asked myself a simple, critical question: What is the most disruptive idea I can possibly come up with? After a while, the answer struck me like a bolt of lightning. I decided to start a women's boxing program.

You're probably thinking I needed to have my head examined. And you're right. A women's boxing program? In Afghanistan?

But I was determined. What better way to prove to the world that Afghanistan was ready for real social change?

I had gotten to know some girls through my soccer programs. During water breaks I showed them how to shadowbox. I would bob and weave and sometimes pummel with the other coaches. The girls thought it was hilarious but it also made them curious about boxing and combat sports. I even had my soccer players shadowbox during warm-ups, not just to get them ready to play but so they could be seen as warriors ready to join my mission. I decided to open up a boxing gym. Finding space wasn't an issue because I had so many friends and family members who owned retail spaces and properties throughout Kabul. I opened up a small boxing gym and asked these girls if they would come train as fighters. They loved it, so we got a few more involved. That made me even more optimistic I could pull this off.

I knew we would eventually need a much larger space, and once again I set my sights on the most disruptive location I could think of: Ghazi National Olympic Stadium, which the Taliban had once used as public execution grounds. The stadium had a private club, and I wanted to secure that for my lady boxers. Thanks to the relationship I had built with Anwar Jekdelek, I was able to make this happen.

I'm not sure I thought of using the stadium as dangerous, but there were definitely risks involved. I told the girls that if I was going to take that risk, I needed them to be all in. They gave me their full commitment. After a couple of months of working them out, I could see that I was onto something truly special, truly disruptive. I wanted to scale it up, but I had to do it the exact right way.

Needless to say, I had a hard time convincing people it could happen. Even my mom said I was taking this one too far. Lots of other people were telling me I couldn't pull it off. The thing I noticed, though, was that they were never stating their own preferences. They kept insisting that it was *other* people, the ones who were running the country, who would stand in my way. I was undeterred. I knew that I was looking at a huge opportunity for disruption. I just had to figure out whom to disrupt.

So I asked everyone: "Who do I have to talk to?"

"The warlords, of course, but they kill you."

"Oh, yeah? Which one? Let me go see him."

I collected names and went down the list, one by one. Then I went to meet them and, as respectfully as I could, tell them what I wanted to do. Each time I heard the same message: "I am willing to help, but others will try to stop you."

Speaking to these supposedly scary people only made me more hopeful. There was one final group I needed to convince— the Taliban. Even though their central leadership was eradicated in the war with the United States after 9/11, the Taliban was still very influential in Afghanistan. If I was going to get this done, I would have to have them on board. Sounds simple, right?

———

I went back to General Malik Zarine and told him what I wanted to do. Of course he thought I was insane. But when I laid out my vision for him, his whole demeanor changed. I remember he was eating food out of a bowl. It was traditional Pashtun shurwa broth with fresh Afghan bread soaked in it, as well as fresh vegetables and herbs like onions, cilantro, tomatoes, and mint. As a gesture of brother-hood he slid the bowl about four inches toward me and invited me to eat from it with him. Then he grabbed my head, kissed my fore-head, and said, "You are the angel that is going to save this country. I control eighty thousand soldiers. You will have our full support."

As I spoke with people about the Taliban, it became apparent that the person I needed to see was a man named Wakil Ahmad Muttawakil. He had formerly served as foreign minister to the Taliban and was also the spokesman and secretary to Mullah Mo-hammed Omar, the Taliban's leader.

I'd be lying if I said I didn't have my moments of doubt. I wanted to be selfless, not suicidal. Going to see Muttawakil would be a risky move. Was it really worth it just to get girls in Afghanistan to box? The more I considered that question, the more I landed on the same answer: Hell yeah. Here was a chance for Afghanistan to make a huge international statement, not just for our own country but for every Islamic Republic across the planet. This was an opportunity to disrupt the social fabric of Islamic society.

The whole equation made me reset my entire relationship with fear. Of course I was afraid, but for the first time in my life I *wanted* to be afraid. It meant I was doing something big and dan-gerous and important. How often does life give you the opportu-nity to be so frightened? Isn't that the very definition of selflessness?

———

Getting in touch with Muttawakil was easier than you might think. Afghanistan is not a big country, and the circles I was dealing with were very tight. Anyone you needed to contact was two phone calls away.

In this case, I reached out to a relative of mine named Ahmad Shaw. I don't even know exactly how he's related to me, but I knew he was heavily influential during the war with the Soviets. I called Ahmad and told him I wanted to be put in contact with Muttawakil.

Ahmad knew exactly who could make that happen. Our family name still carried a lot of weight in Afghanistan, especially among leaders of an older generation. Ahmad put me in touch with someone who was close to Muttawakil. When I called this person, he told me he had already spoken with Wakil and he was expecting to hear from me. Then he gave me the number. It was that easy.

Before I dialed, I had to think it through one last time. I was only twenty-four years old. I wasn't scared for my safety so much as I was worried that I would say the wrong thing and mess everything up. I wanted to be confident without insulting Muttawakil, and I needed to be clear enough that he didn't suspect I was a spy or someone working for an agency that wanted to harm him. It was quite the delicate dance, and I knew full well that my life literally hung in the balance.

Finally, I got my nerve up and dialed. A voice answered. I spoke in Pashto. "Muttawakil Saeb, I am Tareq Azim, the grandson of Shawl Patcha and son of Fazel Azim Patcha. Your number was given to me by your associate Agha Siddiqi. I am from the U.S. but I have been in Afghanistan for two years and I would love to meet with you to discuss an idea that I have."

His reaction was immediate and positive. "It would be an honor, young brother," he said. "You may be my guest at any time."

"What's the soonest I can see you?" I asked.

"You may come tomorrow if that works for you. We will have lunch."

I asked him where he lived. He would only say he was about twenty minutes outside of Kabul. "Your driver will know where I am," he said. I agreed to come, and we hung up.

Suffice to say, I didn't sleep much that night. I paced my living room, replaying the phone call in my mind, searching for any clues to figure out how much danger I was in. Muttawakil's words were friendly but he was very monotone and matter-of-fact—like the Mafia. I started second-guessing myself. Should I just talk him over the phone? Should I invite him to my house instead? I didn't even know exactly where I was going. Just get in a taxi and drop this dude's name? Was I going to end up at his doorstep or with a bag over my head? Worst of all, I couldn't really tell anyone where I was going. That would have made it more dangerous. What if they tipped off one of Muttawakil's enemies? What if they were KGB or Mossad or ISI and I didn't even know it? Like I said, you couldn't trust anyone in that country.

I told only one person, Ahmad Shaw. I knew if there was anyone who could tap into the underground if he needed to and learn my whereabouts, it would be him. I certainly didn't tell my mom. She was worried enough already.

When morning came, I climbed into a taxi. I told the driver where I wanted to go, and just as Muttawakil had predicted, he knew how to get there. As soon as we left downtown Kabul, I started getting anxious. I became paranoid. Why did this driver know right away how to get to Muttawakil's house? Was he working for Muttawakil, or maybe the opposition? I was wearing traditional black Afghan clothing, and I was sweating bullets.

We pulled up to a compound in the middle of nowhere. It was called Khushal Minna. I looked out the window of the taxi and saw all these dudes wearing military outfits and holding guns. They were all over the place. Was one of them going to arrest me? Or kidnap me? For once I wished I had been more selfish. What was wrong with me?

Making me feel even more suspicious was the fact that these guys were not in traditional garb but rather army and police commando uniforms. A guard at the front of the compound waved us to a stop and came to the driver's window. "I have a noon appointment with Wakil Ahmad Muttawakil," I said.

He asked my name, but I was too paranoid to give it. "Does it really matter?" I asked. He replied that it did, so I told him. He checked with some of the other guys and then waved us in.

I walked into the house. A short man came to greet me. He escorted me down a long, dark hallway. I could see some of the side rooms that were empty except for mats on the floor. They reminded me of some of the rooms I had seen in videos of beheadings. My heart raced. When my escort brought me to a room with the maroon couches and closed the door, my fear started to overtake me. Was this whole thing a setup? Was I destined to be in one of those videos?

Finally, after what seemed like an hour but was probably only about fifteen minutes, Muttawakil walked into the room. He looked more like a history professor than some fearsome warlord. He gave me a long greeting and made small talk by asking about my family. He was warm and friendly and quite disarming. I relaxed, but only a little.

As we conversed in our native Pashto, I battled conflicting impulses. I wanted to show confidence, but I also needed to make sure I gave him the proper respect. I didn't want to get too comfortable and accidentally insult him. I talked to him about my family background, which he knew quite well, and the reasons I had come back to Afghanistan. I told him about all the land disputes that were tearing my family apart and how it fueled my desire to stay in the country and try to make things better. We also spoke in Dari and even some English. I was accompanied by a filmmaker who was planning to produce a documentary about my experiences in Afghanistan. His name was Peter Getzels. He was Jewish and wore a Star of David around his neck. Muttawakil remarked amiably about Peter's necklace, but because we weren't speaking in English, Peter didn't know. When I told him later, he just about shit his pants.

I talked to Muttawakil about my experiences in America and how sports worked to bring people together. I was honest about my opinions about Afghanistan. Sometimes he nodded and smiled. Other times he gave me quizzical, even annoyed looks. It was almost like was trying to keep me off-guard. As I was trying to read his reactions, I kept thinking, *This guy is fucking with me.*

Finally, after about forty minutes of conversation, I got to the point of my visit. I took a deep breath and informed him that, based on my experiences witnessing the unifying power of sports in America and its potential to instigate meaningful social change, I wanted to establish a national women's boxing federation in Afghanistan. I started to go into the long explanation I had prepared, laying out how sports aren't just for men, that women should participate as well, even in such a male-dominated sport as boxing, and how it would demonstrate that Afghanistan is really a progressive, peaceful society that has much to offer its citizens and the rest of the world.

Before I could get started with all that explaining, Muttawakil cut me off. "I couldn't agree with you more," he said.

To say I was surprised is an understatement. I mean, I thought I could convince him over time, but I assumed he would at least take *some* convincing. But he didn't. "If people were true students of our faith," he said, "they would understand that we value the significance of women in our society."

At this point, I risked being overly comfortable, but I felt compelled to ask him, "Why does the Taliban oppress women? Why are they not allowed to do anything and always have to be covered up?"

"Young brother," he replied, "let me ask you something. How long have you been in Afghanistan?"

"A little over two years."

"And what do you see?"

"I see a lot of corruption, theft, a total lack of trust. I see no governance. It's a society of savages."

"Exactly," Muttawakil said. "*Savages.*" He went on to explain that before I got there, things had been far worse, despite all the foreign countries coming in and spending billions of dollars there.

"Imagine what it was like when our regime took over following thirty years of war," he said. "The only thing women were being used for was to work in brothels. For generations, women were treated like property. They were objects to be violated, nothing more. Even small girls would be kidnapped and raped like it was nothing. It happened all the time."

This, he said, was the reason the Taliban insisted women wear burkas. He said it was for their protection from attacks of the men around them, that the laws of Islam actually placed a high value on women. He talked about how women have the holy duty of bearing children, and that they must be protected at all times. "The brutality went on for generations," he said. "It will take time to educate the people about these things."

Now let me stop and be clear about something: I am not here to defend the Taliban. I am not asking you to buy his explanation. I understand that in many ways it has been a brutal, violent regime, and I certainly do not condone any support some of its members gave to Al Qaeda. I will note that Muttawakil defected from the Taliban a month after the 9/11 attacks and that before those attacks he had reportedly tried to warn the United States of Al Qaeda's plans. But he is a supporter of the current Taliban's ideology, which includes enforcing Sharia law.

Whatever we know about what the Taliban has done in the past, the fact that Muttawakil reacted to my idea the way he did was very telling. It certainly shocked the hell out of me.

When Muttawakil asked me how I planned to start this program, I told him I already had about a half dozen girls who were in the program, not only to get better at boxing but to prove to the world that Afghanistan was ready for real social change. He was extremely curious and wanted to know how it worked. I explained it to him, and then I laid out my vision of what a national federation would look like. I told him that if we could train competitive female boxers, it would be a great thing for the international perception of the Taliban.

He gave me his full approval, but with one condition: he wanted the women to be dressed in proper accordance with Sharia law. They didn't have to wear burkas, but they should not be showing any skin, could not wear sports bras, and should have their heads covered. I agreed immediately. In my head I was already imagining a deal with Nike to make special Sharia-compliant uniforms.

My meeting with Muttawakil lasted three hours. He encouraged me to come back anytime if I needed more assistance. As the meeting wrapped up, I knew I had everything I needed to get this thing going. I could pitch it to anyone. After all my work, now I had the Taliban in my corner. Who was going to say no to me now?

The Game Plan: Chris James's Selfless Friendship

"Hey, bear!"

The words made the hairs on my neck stand straight up. It had been getting dark in the Grand Teton Mountains, and it was time for the day's hike to come to an end. The scenery was so beautiful—tall mountains, expansive valley, lush forest—all glowing under the last remnants of the setting sun. We were wrapping up for the day and making our way back to our camp.

That's when I heard those two ominous words from Ron, our hunting partner and guide. *"Hey, bear!"* I was standing next to my other hunting partner, Chris James. We turned around and saw what Ron had seen: a grizzly bear, four paws on the ground, facing us and giving every indication he was ready to charge. I felt as if I were looking right at death—and believe me, I wasn't smiling.

I was frozen for a second but Chris didn't hesitate. He grabbed my neck and said, "Let's go!" We started running full speed at Ron. It seemed like we were moving in slow motion, but it was a fifteen-foot sprint with a leap over three feet of logs and brush. Nothing was in our minds except saving Ron. By the time we got to him, the bear's front paws had come back to the ground. He turned broadside to us so we could see how big he was and disappeared into the woods.

We had no idea if the bear had really left or was just circling and getting ready to charge back. We only knew for sure we had to get out of there. Chris got in Ron's face and worked to calm him down. He knew Ron's adrenaline was pulsing like crazy. The three of us pressed our backs together and pushed our way through the woods like a bunch of ninjas. It took us a little over an hour to make it back to camp and feel like we were out of the woods, so to speak.

Besides being one of my closest friends, Chris is a husband and father of three children. At the time he was also the founder and managing partner of Partner Fund Management, a Silicon Valley–based hedge fund that managed around $5 billion in assets. Suffice to say, he had a lot to lose if things had gone wrong in that encounter with that bear, yet as I said, he never hesitated to do the selfless thing.

It wasn't until much later when I was able to calm down and replay what happened that I allowed myself to be amazed at Chris's poise in that situation. Not that it surprised me. Chris embodies the very concept of selflessness, and his actions in that moment proved once again that just because you put others before yourself doesn't have to make you a sucker in life or in business. If anything, it can help you become even more successful, however you choose to define that word. Chris is a black belt when it comes to managing his hedge fund, but his selflessness is his greatest asset.

———

Unlike a lot of people in his industry, Chris has been very intentional about staying out of the spotlight. It's not in his nature to seek attention, and he wants to protect his kids, not only from public scrutiny but also from having to live in his shadow. And he has absolutely zero ego when it comes to claiming credit.

Chris is the most motivated teammate I've ever had. We met in early 2012, when he became the first person to work out at Empower. He was tall and skinny, about six-four and 177 pounds, but I could tell how intense he was by the way he shook my hand. He told me he had been boxing for four years, so I suggested we lace up the gloves and do some bag work. He was doing a lot of things wrong, starting with the way he taped his hands. As the workout progressed, I changed his mechanics to show him how to use his hips and body weight in order to throw a more powerful jab. I pinched his love handles and said, "Hey, man, it's okay to smile in here."

I was geeked up about the idea of training this interesting new client. And then . . . nothing. Not a word. For three months. I had never had a client just blow me off like that. I felt like a jilted lover.

Finally, his office called Empower and asked to set up another session. When my booker told me this, I told her to forget it. Chris's office kept calling, and we kept ignoring him. One day I was in training camp for an upcoming UFC fight and Chris showed up. I tried to blow him off, but he was persistent. "What's going on?" he asked. "Why can't I get in with you?" I told him I didn't appreciate how he had ghosted me. "Are you serious?" he said. He lifted up his shirt to reveal a large scar across his shoulder and a second one on his knee. He had had a bad injury from a skiing accident a while back, and he finally decided to go under the knife. That's why he didn't smile that first day when his jabs were landing. He was in too much pain. "All the time I was doing rehab, you were my motivation," he said.

I felt so bad. It was like we were in couples therapy. I gave him a hug and told the front desk that anytime Chris called, he should get an appointment immediately.

From that point on, we worked out almost every day. We'd do strength and conditioning three days a week and then box for the rest. Chris would sometimes do double days to include additional boxing and Jiu Jitsu. He gave me permission to push him, and I watched him embrace the pain. Within about eighteen months he was up to 203 pounds and grappling with Jake Shields and some of my other top MMA fighters. I would focus on hitting his body, which made it difficult for him to breathe. Or I'd pin him with my elbow on his chest to take some air out of him. The purpose as always was to help him learn to be comfortable with discomfort.

Chris has a burning desire to be excellent at whatever he does. He has become, pound for pound, as strong as anyone that I train. We got him to bench-press over 300 pounds, much more than he had ever pressed in his life. He was also rowing a couple of times a week. By the end of our first year together, he was by far in the best shape of his life. We had a great rapport but it was strictly business. All that time, I had no idea how successful he was.

———

Chris grew up in Harrisburg, Illinois, a small coal mining town in the northern part of the state. His graduating high school class had fewer than two hundred students. Nearly all of them went straight to work in the mines or attended a junior college or vocational school. Only three went on to a four-year college. Chris was one of them. He went to Tulane and majored in economics.

Why was Chris able to beat such staggering odds? Simple: his parents always told him he was going to college, and he believed them. Both of Chris's paternal grandparents went to the University of Illinois, which gave them exposure to a bigger world than what their friends and neighbors saw in Harrisburg. Like me, Chris knows the value—and responsibility—of a grandparent's legacy.

After Chris graduated from Tulane, he moved to New York without any employment lined up. He talked his way into a marketing position at a hedge fund. Six months later he became an analyst. Then, in the mid-1990s, the Internet exploded. When Netscape held its incredibly lucrative IPO, Chris decided to move to San Francisco and try to ride the tech wave. Needless to say, that turned out to be a very smart business decision. He eventually became an executive at Pequot Capital and then started PFM in 2004.

Chris is a very guarded person. He operates in a world where everyone he meets wants something from him. That's why he lets so few people into his inner circle. After a year of working together, he invited me to have dinner with him at Tosca Cafe in San Francisco. He was very curious to learn about me, so I shared with him some of the details of my family and my upbringing. We started talking about my business and where I wanted to go with it. He was giving me some pointers and asked, "Do you know what I do?"

"No," I replied.

"I run a hedge fund," he said. "We invest in people and companies.

To that point, I hadn't thought much about Chris's work life. Was I impressed by his achievements? Of course. But it's not like I was blinded by his wealth. Remember, I came from a family that at one time was extremely wealthy. I don't have a huge fascination with money like a lot of people do. From the time I was young I was conscious not to define success by my ability to collect things. What's the point? None of it belongs to you. None of it goes to your grave. It's not really yours, so why be so protective about it? Why not put that energy instead into what's actually yours, which is your legacy, your impact, and your ability to impact others through selflessness?

The more Chris learned about my family history, the more he wanted to know. He listened raptly as I talked about my grandfather and parents and the years I spent in Afghanistan. I got emotional as I always do when talking about all that stuff, and I confessed to Chris the fears and pressure I feel every day to live up to that legacy. He could see that, for all my macho posturing, I was not hesitant about exposing my vulnerability. This drew us even closer.

It wasn't long before Chris and I became fast friends. He came to family functions, and in return he invited me to dinners and parties. I got to know his wife and his boys. His boys call me "Uncle T-Man." I love those boys. When our fathers passed away, Chris and I were there for each other every step of the way.

Our relationship went to another level in 2014, when I was getting ready to raise some capital to expand my business. I was getting advice on how to go about it from a group of his colleagues. At one point one of them said to me, "You should ask C.J. to participate. You know he would do anything for you." I told them I appreciated the suggestion, but that I knew that Empower was one of the few places Chris could go in his life where he did not have any financial interest, and I wanted to keep it that way. That's why I also stopped billing him for our workouts, even though he could obviously afford them. I know how many financial obligations Chris has, and I don't want to be one of them. Our relationship is built on selflessness. It's rare to have someone in your life whose friendship could never be replaced by any amount of money. I would never do anything to jeopardize that.

———

Chris and I almost always do our work in late afternoons, between his hours at the office and his time at home. In the past, Chris had difficulty shedding his office persona so he could be present the way he needed to be at home. Our workouts became a way for him to transition from the office, where he's the boss, to his home, where he's definitely not. He knew he needed to be humbled, and there are few things more humbling than trying to learn something new.

That process was very similar to the transition I went through on that emotional car ride from the airport in Kabul to my father's house. Chris's work at Empower became his bridge from being *selfish* to *selfless*. From being the Man in Charge to being Dad. He needs to honor both aspects of his personality, but he can't be both things at once. This is what all of us face on a daily basis.

I've teased Chris that when he's in the office, I'll bet he's the type to throw a clock against the wall when he gets angry. But that was just my mistaken impression. The truth is he has never thrown anything, but he does like to say that capitalism is a contact sport. He is a self-described skeptic. If someone comes to him with a business idea, Chris sees it as his job to create friction in an effort to figure out whether this company is worth a major investment.

There were times he would try to bring that mind-set into our workouts. Then it was my turn to set the tone. "Hey, man, that shit don't work in here," I'd say. "You're in *my* office now." Chris is used to people treating him with kid gloves once they find out he's loaded. He never has to worry about that with me or any of his teammates at Empower, whom we call the Stable of Champions. If we're sparring or grappling and he tries to really challenge me, I go into grizzly mode, as we call it. I actually can't help myself. He pops me one good time, and it's *on*. We laugh about it afterward, but I warn him, "You're my friend and I love you, but I'm not your fucking punching bag."

Chris doesn't want me to hurt him, of course, but he does want me to test him. That line can get blurry, but that's where we live. It takes a special kind of personality to seek out discomfort. That doesn't make Chris a masochist. There's a big difference. Chris wants to be challenged and pressed. He knows it's the only way to conquer the disease of fear.

Someone once gave Chris some very good financial advice that I think applies to a lot of areas in life: The stock markets are not the place where you should find out who you really are. You need to find that out *before* you get into the market. This is how physical training should work as well. You get punched, you feel pain, you have a hard time breathing, and you find out who you are. Then you go out into the world and honor that truth.

Chris knows that the most important variable in whether a business succeeds is not the idea, it's the execution. It's like being a boxer. You can have a good game plan all you want, but if you can't pull it off in the ring, you're going to end up flat on the canvas. This is why Chris has to stay selfish *and* selfless.

————

Chris took his commitment to selflessness to another level in December 2020, when he announced he was launching a new firm called Engine No. 1, which invests in companies that will perform better financially if they improve their performance in the areas of environmental and social impact. Besides requiring time and money, the new firm will also force Chris to adopt a more public persona. He built his wealth on his ability to see the future. Now he wants that future to be cleaner, healthier, and more selfless.

It's funny, because people look at me and Chris sometimes and ask: "Why are you guys so close?" On the surface we seem so different, but underneath we have much in common. Chris and I do just about everything together you can think of. If he's not training in my gym, we're hanging out, going on surfing and skiing trips, or spending time with each other's families. He knows me as well as anyone.

Because selflessness is the foundation of our relationship, we are able to be completely honest with each other. Chris is never hesitant to call me out when I need it. He's never concerned about losing my friendship, because he knows I'm not going anywhere. He's also not afraid to tell me when he thinks I am doing things wrong with my businesses or in my personal life. He is always pushing me to scale what I do and not take things so personally. That's why, even though he himself shies away from the media, he encouraged me to do that *ESPN The Magazine* article. I had been putting off the writer, Paul Kix, for months, but Chris convinced me I had something valuable to say. I called Paul and told him I had decided to do the story. It was one of the best decisions I ever made.

It was important for me to hear him talk about scaling my business, because up to that point it was something I'd resisted.

The bigger my businesses got, the more responsibilities I took on, and because I often put other people ahead of myself, that made me fearful of disrupting things. I became many of the things I am pushing against in this book—afraid of change, reluctant to give myself permission to grow, hesitant to realize my truth, holding big dreams but deep down not wanting to succeed. Chris often tells me I am doing way too many things. He's one of the few people in my life who can say, "You're the only reason you're not doing you."

Chris worries about me a lot. He knows that I have had three back surgeries, and yet he sees me out there pumping iron, sparring and grappling with world champions, pushing my body to the limit. He has told me that I need to be careful about getting trapped in a persona and putting myself in a bad position just because I want to look like someone who trains NFL players and elite operators. He's right, but the thing is, I don't feel things the way other people do. I believe you can struggle and hurt and push your mind and body past their limits and still feel like you are in your comfort zone.

The same can be said for the way I take on my family legacy, which is another one of Chris's concerns. I try to tell him that my legacy is built into my intentions. Take that away, and it's like taking away my base. It might look from the outside like I am in pain, but this is what I am conditioned to feel like. It's like if someone told you to run ten miles real fast, it would crush you. But if you trained every day for a year and got your body into the proper condition, you could bang out those ten miles with ease. I'm not worried this burden is going to crush me because I don't believe in crushing. This is my choice. It's the feeling I want to have.

This is how it is with me and Chris. We can tell each other the truth and point out the ways we are holding ourselves back, and in the next breath laugh in acknowledgment that we have the same exact faults. Yes, we are achievers who seek pain and discomfort because we know that is the only way to honor our truths. Yet, we must never forget that the whole purpose of that pain is so we can serve others. Most of all, we know we can never let our sense of ourselves and our definition of success be tied to specific outcomes.

Chris and I stick together because we remind each other of this every day. We know that unless we find our way across that bridge to selflessness, we can never truly conquer the disease of fear.

CHAPTER SEVEN

DISCOMFORT

My long-term stay in Afghanistan began in 2004, but I came back to the States every few months so I could see my family and take care of some business. I still thought I could be a professional Mixed Martial Arts fighter, so I trained my ass off with some of the best fighters in the MMA game. Little did I know that in doing so, I was acquiring the knowledge and relationships that would give me a brand-new life.

While working out with local guys in the Bay Area, I was introduced to an up-and-coming Italian fighter named Alessio Sakara, whom I met in Los Angeles. Alessio and I were about the same size, and though his boxing skills were way ahead of mine, I more than held my own when we sparred. One day he asked if I would be his training partner for his upcoming fight. Hell yeah I would! In time, I became more of a coach than a partner. I didn't really know what I was doing, but Alessio and I bounced ideas off each other and tried new things. It was tough and exhausting, but we had fun.

I went with Alessio to his fight in Las Vegas in 2005. It was the first time I had experienced a big-time UFC event. It was so powerful and energizing, especially when Alessio won. I continued to help him train and worked his corner on fight nights. One of those was a UFC card at Staples Center in Los Angeles. I had never been a part of a fight that big. He did a ton of interviews and press conferences in the week leading up to the fight. On the night of the event, we were warming up backstage and all these cameras were around. Before we went out, Alessio put a gladiator necklace on me. We walked out and I saw Cindy Crawford and other celebrities sitting near the cage. Alessio lost that night, but I was hooked on everything about the experience.

On another one of my trips home from Afghanistan, I reached out to Mike Bruno, the managing director at the Fairtex gym in San Francisco. Mike mentored a lot of prestigious fighters, so I told him I wanted to come there to work out. That's where I got involved with big-time fighters like Jake Shields, Gilbert Melendez, and Josh McDonald. They were doing some Muay Thai boxing, which is a style of fighting that comes from Thailand. It's basically boxing with a lot of clinching techniques. Muay Thai is known as the "art of eight limbs" because it involves shins, knees, elbows, and fists.

Josh McDonald asked me for help, especially with his stand-up boxing and movements, which was my expertise. We worked together for about a month. He taught me a lot about wrestling, and I taught him about stand-up. Some of the other guys were away during that time, but when they came back they noticed a change in Josh. Jake Shields wanted to do some of the same work.

We started messing around with different techniques, and I told him my understanding of the fundamentals of footwork and jabs. Jake's love for stand-up went through the roof. We became teammates.

This was my first discovery group, my first incubator. All these different ideas came together at once. Josh was the best at wrestling. Jake was the best at Jiu Jitsu. I excelled at stand-up. Gilbert was tops at Mixed Martial Arts. Luke Stewart, who was a renowned black belt in Jiu Jitsu, was also in the group. We would work out for hours, experimenting and mixing together all of these elements. It was the best education I could get.

I would work with this group of champions for four to six weeks and then head back to Afghanistan. We stayed in touch through texts and MySpace, and they would ask when I was coming back. Jake had a big fight in Los Angeles Coliseum and wanted me to train him. So I returned to the States for another six weeks. I had never coached anyone full-time before, much less for such a major bout. But I had gained so much knowledge from all those group sessions at Fairtex, I was developing my confidence.

My curiosity was insatiable. I went online and researched a famous Russian fighter named Fedor Emilanko, who had a drill where he spun around on a broomstick, got real dizzy, and then sparred. So I brought in a broomstick to Fairtex, handed it to Jake, got him real dizzy, and then pounded the shit out of him. We still laugh about that to this day, but it was an example of how we used trial and error to build our fundamentals, enhance our practice, and find out what really worked. It was crazy, man. I had never done anything like this before, and here was this world-class fighter who was giving me his total trust. There was no way I was going to let him regret that.

At the same time, I was not giving up on my own dreams of a fight career. Mike Bruno was busting his butt trying to get me fights, but while I got some smaller opportunities with local shows and fight leagues that were in development, things would always fall through. In the end, my back problems undermined my chances just as they had derailed my NFL dreams. But it was a pretty good consolation prize to work with someone like Jake Shields, which gave me the chance to learn every day from one of the best fighters in the world. He and Josh both told me they thought my true calling was to help them win world championships, so that's what I dedicated myself toward doing.

As I look back on those years, I can see how my discomfort set me on a greater path. I experienced intense disappointment when presented with my physical limitations, but I still pressed on with the training and coaching. It was uncomfortable to concede that I was never going to be a big-time fighter, but if I hadn't gotten hurt again, perhaps Jake and Luke and the rest of that crew would have found someone else to coach them. My whole life would have turned out differently. I saw that my purpose in this world was to help others push through discomfort and achieve the benefits of competition.

In a broader sense, I learned something of real importance from those fighters: the only way to win in the ring is to *be* in the ring. That means you not only have to tolerate discomfort but chase it. This is an unnatural instinct for most people. We spend our entire lives avoiding pain. As a result, we get complacent and feel stuck. We stop growing. We stop fighting.

We succumb to the disease of fear.

You see these great big fighters with their chiseled physiques and lethal techniques, and you just assume they are steel on the inside. I'm here to tell you that they're not. The truth is, they're scared shitless. I mean, they are entering a confined space with another man whose entire purpose in life is to hurt them so badly that they end up unconscious. It is a *highly* uncomfortable situation. Yet, every day of their lives, they step into that ring and meet that discomfort head-on. The truth is, they couldn't live their truths without it.

––––––

It is amazing to think how much angst we cause ourselves by trying to avoid discomfort. This makes zero sense. We're much better off building a relationship with fear. That's how we conquer the disease.

Why is fear so paralyzing? I believe it's because fear is where the heart and head intersect. We get stuck because we are trying to put those things into a blender and assign them the same responsibilities, as if the emotional answer is the same as a mental answer or a physical answer. Rather, each of those parts has its own ability to process fear and discomfort. When we allow ourselves to experience these emotions, a natural synchronization takes place. It's not something we need to force.

When your heart and head come together in the face of fear, then you will know what it means to experience unconditional love. Everything is working together. The head knows all about your expectations and disappointments. The heart knows all about your frustrations and anger. If we are too dominant with one facet, then we make things overly complicated. It makes life a lot harder than it needs to be. We try to manipulate thoughts and emotions, which only feeds our insecurities when we find we are unable to do this.

Instead of all this manipulating and avoiding, we need to embrace discomfort. With embracing comes trust. With trust comes gratitude.

What do I mean by fear? I get asked this a lot and my answer is always the same: You tell me. The answer comes through your daily practice. You don't need to write about it, you don't need to post about it on social media. You just need to confront it. Don't allow someone else to set this narrative. You choose to define what fear means to you. It's no different from choosing to wear a white shirt or a dark one. How do you want to feel today?

For me, fear is a pathway to consciousness. If I'm fearful of something, that's making me conscious that it needs attention. If thinking about what frightens you causes discomfort, that's okay, too. This is something that is happening internally. How can you apply your definition of fear to the situation? What's happening in my world? Am I going to be able to pay the rent? Am I going to be able to feed my family? Will my business stay open? Will this pandemic end so I can travel to see my loved ones again?

Don't feel bad if you have fallen into these traps. Believe me, I'm as guilty as anyone. I can easily go down the rabbit hole of being super negative. That's when I try to use that feeling to feed my consciousness. I'm one of the most emotional people you will meet. I suffer from great insecurity. So I am constantly seeking discomfort in order to work on my relationship with fear. I can overcome it in a certain moment, but then it comes back. What then?

When I start to go into this negative thinking, I very intentionally recognize it and work to change my mind-set. That means focusing intently on my words and my language. One thing I've come to appreciate over the years is the power of words. They can add to your mental baggage or make you feel lighter. Same with thoughts. So when you feel yourself headed this way, try to start imagining best-case scenarios. Think of something that will never allow your eyebrows to sink. Think about things that will allow you to sleep peacefully and breathe easily.

My challenge to you is to figure out how valuable fear is to you. The first step is to identify what fear means. Step two is identifying deficiencies in your day-to-day life that bring about this fear. Don't think about anything other than the here and now. Think about how to prepare yourself for this moment, which is meant for your survival. Then you're ready for step three, which is to allow yourself to experience discomfort so you can build that relationship with fear and the unknown.

When I was younger, I tied my identity to my physical abilities, but when my body broke down, I had to face my limitations. Over time, I realized that I was making the mistake of viewing life through a purely physical lens. I learned to see things through other people's thoughts and emotions. The same things that make a person a great leader in a locker room also work in the boardroom, or in a family. As Albert Einstein said, "Adversity introduces a man to himself." Discomfort is a precursor to growth, physically and emotionally. We can't "level up" if we are too comfortable.

You might not think it's that easy, but oftentimes it is. The important thing to remember is that you have freedom. It's the freedom to keep your positive thoughts stimulated. Use it! Physically we can do push-ups and jumping jacks and crunches all day long. Why would we do that for our limbs and not our hearts?

I can't say it's something I planned or intended, but the theme of discomfort would dominate the remainder of my stay in Afghanistan. That country does not let a person become comfortable. Your life is in danger every moment, to the point where you are basically resigned to it. You think, *If I die today, I die, but it's not going to stop me from living.* Fear is your constant companion. You can succumb to the disease, or you can build a relationship with it.

This tension was especially apparent during my visits to the U.S. military bases. I loved going to those bases because they gave me a great taste of home—literally so, since I often went because I was craving Burger King, a decent cup of coffee, or some Thousand Island dressing on my salad. It was like a Little America. The military welcomed me for a variety of reasons, not least because the biggest base there, the Bagram Air Base, was started by my grandfather. I'd eat with the soldiers and Navy SEALs and they'd hear me talk and see my mangled ears and want to know more about what I was doing in the States. I taught them martial arts and told them about my family and my lady boxers in Afghanistan. Then I'd go home for a while and they'd see me on TV coaching Jake Shields and get a big kick out of that.

That level of trust, respect, and familiarity lowered the waterline between us. In turn, they opened up to me about what they were thinking and feeling. I tried to share with them what I knew about the people around Afghanistan. There was just so much misunderstanding and distrust between the two sides. "These people don't want to kill you," I told them. "You don't need to be so fearful of them."

This came as a major surprise, so I tried to address this wide gulf between their opinions and the truth on the ground. The best success happened with a PRT (provincial reconstruction team) that worked out of a satellite base on the outskirts of Tora Bora. It was a smaller base of about two hundred soldiers, sitting on thirty acres with the entrance located at the end of a long driveway. The soldiers there were absolutely terrified of the people who lived on the other side of that driveway. I brought my mom there and the soldiers thought we were extremely valuable, because they knew we were Americans who came from Afghan families of influence and relevance during the monarchy. That gave us a lot of leverage with both sides.

We convinced a group of soldiers to go with us on a visit to the place where my mom was building a private school, which was located in one of the most dangerous areas in Nengrahar Province. I'll never forget the sight of six American Humvees pulling into this school sitting in a valley surrounded by mountains full of Al Qaeda and the Taliban. It required a willingness to be vulnerable, which created trust between the soldiers and that community.

The soldiers were greeted with open arms. The locals presented them with gifts, food, and hugs. The entire narrative of their relationship shifted before my eyes. The Americans realized that for all the dangers, there was a large portion of the Afghan population that loved that they were in the country and wanted them to be safe. It blew them away.

Such is the nature of fear. It often requires misunderstandings and incorrect assumptions. The Americans visited many more times, including the opening of the school, when they brought backpacks full of notebooks, pens, and pencils.

I also maintained a lot of the relationships I formed in the military throughout my time in Afghanistan. In 2007, I was invited to teach hand-to-hand fighting to U.S. troops in Iraq. I did a ten-day seminar with members of the Third Special Forces Group. There was a lot of downtime where I got to know the soldiers. Since I always speed-drive conversations into real talk, I heard a lot about their struggles with mental health, even if they wouldn't have described them that way. I thought to myself, *Man, there are a lot of guys hurting here.*

It was quite an environment I was operating in. I wanted to disrupt all that fear and discomfort, but there was so much of it, I felt overwhelmed much of the time. I decided to focus on things I could control, beginning with the program I wanted to build for my boxers. Those women had become all too accustomed to living lives that had lots of discomfort but not enough purpose. Every day for them was a battle with the disease of fear. So I taught them to respond the only way I knew how—by fighting.

———

Once I got approval from Wakil Muttawakil and the Taliban to form my women's boxing federation, things happened very quickly.

I had lunch with my counterparts from the women's sports federation as well as someone from the Afghan men's boxing federation. When I explained to them what I had done, their eyes got huge. They couldn't believe we had the support of Taliban warlords!

My next big meeting was with Anwar Jekdelek, the president of the Afghan Olympic federation. He had fought side by side with a few of my uncles against the Soviet occupation, so we had an instant connection. When I went to his lavish office on the third floor of the Ghazi Stadium Olympic headquarters, we had some tea, and I told him about my meeting with Muttawakil and what I had already done with females in my boxing club. Right away he said, "Anything you want to do in this country, you have my blessings." He picked up a phone and instructed his chief of staff to prepare a statement announcing the creation of the Afghan women's boxing federation. I told him it would not be easy for me to find a space to work out my fighters. He said he had a space downstairs in his building. Done and done.

As we wrapped up our meeting, I looked outside and saw two of my lady boxers who were waiting to learn how it went. I walked outside and announced, "We're a federation!" We celebrated.

Still, there were major challenges ahead. A big problem that Afghanistan has always faced is that no one believes peace is profitable. That's why I felt like I couldn't trust anyone, especially government officials. Why would they want prosperity and peace when there are so many companies trying to get contracts to rebuild and provide security? But I knew from my experiences that things like national parks and big sports events can be drivers of economic activity. To break through, you have to be more than a visionary. You have to be a disruptor.

I was also able to convince Fairtex to sign on as a sponsor. They sent me a ton of equipment to get us going. Once I had our facility set up, I was able to put the word out about what we were doing. There were many journalists from all over the world working in Afghanistan, and I had gotten to know a few of them. That helped build momentum.

On the other hand, that progress brought out of the woodwork a lot of opportunists, warlords, gangsters, and con artists who wanted to take a bite out of what we were building. It also subjected us to the bullshit that often comes with bureaucracies and big organizations, where everyone is more concerned with protecting their turf than creating meaningful change. It's what happens when people in power are allowed to get comfortable. Navigating through all that became a source of endless frustration for me.

The thing that kept me going through all of that was my girls—my fighters. There was one girl named Fahima, who was the oldest of three sisters in my group. She had a strong presence. I put her in many situations where she had to fight through discomfort, and she always persevered. She was a powerful hitter.

One day I decided to make Fahima team captain. You could see her demeanor change immediately. She was still tough and stern, but she took full responsibility for the team. She took it upon herself to encourage the other girls to push through their own discomfort. If they had transportation issues, Fahima saw to it that they still made it to the stadium. The girls lived all over the city, so it wasn't always easy for them to get there, considering Kabul was originally designed for a population of about three hundred thousand people but held some nine million.

Fahima didn't have any grand ambitions as a boxer, but she understood what we were trying to accomplish in terms of bringing about social change. Her sister, Shabnam, on the other hand, had real chops as a boxer. It was hard to see it at first. She was this little princess. Every time she threw a good jab and it landed with a loud *pop!* she would cover her mouth and giggle, almost embarrassed by what she had done. But I could see she had talent. It wasn't long before she was the top female boxer in Afghanistan.

Once we were under the umbrella of the national federation, the program spread throughout the country. This thing I had started in such a small way had grown fast, but I was happy to let someone else take charge of it. There were too many "officials" who had their grubby hands in it. I found them to be lazy, arrogant, and totally lacking the knowledge they needed. They had no concept of the economic and social potential I had laid at their doorsteps. If anything, they would go out of their way to keep it from growing too big. Maybe if it really took off, they would lose control of it, and in turn they could lose control of other things as well. I am also convinced that even though many people told me to my face that they wanted to see positive social change in Afghanistan, in truth they really wanted women to have a subservient place in society, totally without empowerment.

Our ultimate ambition was to place one or more fighters in the 2012 Olympics in London, where women's boxing was going to make its debut as an Olympic sport. Shabnam was the country's best hope. She had turned into a monster. I would get pictures sent to me from friends who were training her. One of them was of an opponent of hers who had a broken nose. So much for the little princess! I was convinced she was headed for international stardom if she could be a factor at the Olympics. I even started to talk to the UFC about getting Ronda Rousey involved to help spread the word that this young Afghan girl was ready to change the world, one jab at a time.

In the end, Shabnam did not fight in the Olympics, and neither did any other woman from Afghanistan. I am honestly not sure what happened, but I have my suspicions. There was only so much change that the country was willing to tolerate, or at least only at a certain pace. But I have not lost my hope for the future. I have seen firsthand the strength and determination of young Afghan women, and how they respond when they are finally empowered to work hard, follow their dreams, and create the change they seek. The old men who run Afghanistan should not underestimate these women. I know them very, very well. They are not going to let a little discomfort stop them from putting up a good fight.

The Game Plan: Justin Tuck's Comfort with Discomfort

The limitations of my body prevented me from pursuing my NFL dreams, but I was able to live them vicariously through my close friend Dave Tollefson. I was so proud of the career he had built for himself with the New York Giants. I got to know some of his teammates and coaches. One of them was Justin Tuck, a defensive end from Notre Dame.

Dave and Justin were both defensive linemen, which meant they often competed for playing time. If one of them was in the game, the other was probably on the sideline. Normally that causes friction, but not only did Dave and Justin get along, they became blood brothers. I mean this literally—they cut their palms and shook hands on it. They had so much in common. They were both humble and loved the outdoors. They were honest and devoted to their families. And they were the ultimate teammates. When I visited Dave in New York, I got a chance to meet Justin a couple of times.

Tuck, as he is often called, was entering his tenth NFL season in 2014 when he signed a two-year, $11 million free agent contract with the Oakland Raiders. Since I was in the Bay Area, we hooked up right away. It didn't take long for me and Justin to build up the same level of brotherhood. The Raiders had a hotel set up for him next to their facility, but for the first month Justin stayed with me so he could be closer to Empower. Justin knew he was getting toward the end of his career, but he believed he had a couple of good years left. He had dealt with a lot of injuries, so getting himself game-ready, both mentally and physically, was his top priority.

When Tuck first walked into Empower, he expected it would be filled mostly with pro athletes. He was surprised to see an eclectic community of people. It also didn't take long for him to realize he was in for more than he bargained for. He was never the type who felt he needed a trainer to show him what to do. He just wanted someone who would hold him accountable and help him stay in shape.

So he was a little surprised when the first thing I asked him to do was sit with me so we could develop a game plan. I broke down all his goals regarding how much weight he wanted to put on, what he wanted his body fat to be, all that stuff. We did the standard measurements. Then I hit him with one of my core philosophies. "If you want to reach your goals," I said, "you're going to have to learn to be comfortable with discomfort."

At that point, Tuck made the mistake of telling me about a few things that made him uncomfortable. For example, he told me he hated running hills. I smiled, knowing that would go right to the top of our to-do list. I explained it to him this way: "I want to see you walking on water. Then you're going to sink down to your waist, and then your chest. Then the water is going to be at your neck, and finally you'll be *under* the water, but you will force yourself to find peace with it." I was only speaking in a metaphor, but little did I know that Tuck actually couldn't swim. So my metaphor made him freak out a little. We were off to a very uncomfortable start, which is how I like it.

It dawned on Tuck that I was about more than bench presses and squats. It was my job to prepare him, not just physically but mentally and spiritually, for those awful moments when it's late in the fourth quarter and he's at the end of his rope but has to keep fighting with offensive linemen. The natural instinct in those moments is to chase harder, but I wanted to teach Tuck how to slow himself down and manage the discomfort.

Needless to say, the next day I took Tuck to run hills. This was San Francisco, so there were plenty to choose from. It was so hilarious, I thought he was going to fight me. Running hills is particularly good for disrupting breathing patterns. It creates a mentality that doesn't come naturally to the surface; it has to be forced there. But because we had our game plan, he understood my purpose. I wasn't trying to get him to be stronger or faster on those hills. I was trying to get him to be more comfortable with discomfort.

———

Tuck grew up in Kellyton, Alabama, as one of seven children. It was a small town, and it seemed like everyone who lived there had the surname Tuck. It was not unusual for him to spend weekends with forty or fifty relatives at a time. He could never do anything wrong as a kid because he knew someone was always watching. This was similar to the Afghan community that surrounded me when I was young. So despite our surface differences—he was a Black man from rural Alabama, I was the son of Afghan refugees from San Francisco—it felt like we were destined to be close friends.

It started with the deep respect and responsibility we felt for our grandfathers' legacies. Tuck's grandfather, Leroy, exuded brute strength. Justin grew up listening to his granddad tell stories about what it was like to be a sharecropper. Leroy farmed his own land and had multiple jobs on the side to support his family. Tuck has been an all-pro NFL lineman, but he'll tell you he was nowhere near as strong as Leroy.

And yet, the rock of Tuck's family was his grandmother. Like me, he was raised to appreciate the concept of feminine strength. (He also learned this from his older sisters, who used to tape his arms when he was real young, then put him in a trash can and roll him down a hill for fun.) Both of Justin's parents worked long hours, so on many days the school bus would drop him off at his grandmother's house. He learned to cook without using a measuring cup. She talked to him about his family history while they watched the TV game show *Jeopardy!* together.

Most of all, the thing that united me and Tuck was that his dad was also his hero. Jimmy Lee Tuck is a skinny fellow, but he's one of those people who walk into a room and, without even trying, draw everyone's attention with their stature. Tuck will tell you that Jimmy was the real athlete of the family. He played football, baseball, and basketball, and ran track. Tuck often heard stories from people in town about his father's athletic exploits.

On Sundays, Tuck went to Sunday school, followed by a church service, followed by a second service at a different church, and then perhaps a church lunch or a picnic with relatives at home. He became a Sunday school instructor himself at a very young age. He would leave church and look back inside and see his father talking cheerfully to a group of people. He'd ask his dad how he knew those folks, and his father would reply, "I don't. We just met."

Tuck was so big as a child, he gave himself the nickname "He-Man" in honor of his favorite cartoon character. One of the great blessings of his life was that he was raised to revere education. His mother fostered in him a deep love of books. He'll never forget one time when his mother was telling his sister how many friends she had. "You have so many friends," her mom said. "Your math book, your science book, your history book . . ." Justin might be watching TV with his mom and see something about Paris and tell her he wanted to go there someday. "You can go anywhere you want to in a book," his mom would answer. Later, when Tuck was with the Giants, he started an organization called RUSH for Literacy. (That stands for Read, Understand, Succeed, and Hope.) He did a lot of work for the Boys & Girls Clubs and other charities, and in 2011 he coauthored a children's book called *Home-Field Advantage*.

Tuck was fortunate to get the chance to play for Notre Dame—an assistant coach spotted him when he was in town to scout another player—but when he left for South Bend in the fall of 2001, it was the first time he had ever been on a plane. You can imagine how uncomfortable that was. Tuck spent much of his freshman year calling his family and saying he wanted to come home, but his parents wouldn't hear of it.

Those parents raised very high achievers. One of Justin's sisters went to Yale for both undergraduate and medical school. She is now a neurosurgeon at Duke University Hospital. Justin has another brother who is an engineer for Alabama Power, another who is an executive at Verizon. Yet another sister is a schoolteacher, another is a nurse. Tuck was so successful with Notre Dame football that he earned the nickname the "Freak." He graduated as the school's all-time sack leader and was selected by the Giants in the third round of the 2005 NFL Draft. Three years later, he signed a five-year, $30 million contract. Justin played so well when the Giants beat the Patriots in Super Bowl XLII that a lot of people said he should have been named MVP over Eli Manning. He won another Super Bowl ring four years later, and in 2008 and 2010 he made the Pro Bowl.

As Justin became a highly successful and very well-paid NFL defensive lineman, he naturally wanted to share his blessings with his family. But his father wouldn't let him. Every time Justin tried to buy his dad something or send him money, the answer was a very firm "No, thank you." Justin has wired money directly into his father's bank account, only to see it sit there forever or find out that he donated it to some church or other worthy cause. He bought his dad a truck once, but he wouldn't drive it. Justin's parents still live in the same house where he grew up.

That hasn't stopped Justin from trying. One time he conspired with his brother to build their dad a brand-new house. They acquired some property close by, had the land cleared, and hired a contractor to perform a land survey and lay the foundation. Somehow their dad got suspicious and started asking questions. Justin and his brother tried to pass along their concocted story, but their dad smelled a rat. "If you're building this house to give it to me," he said, "I'm gonna burn it down."

Suffice to say, the house never got built. Jimmy Lee Tuck might not have had much by way of material things, but he was very comfortable keeping things as they were.

———

My mom took in Tuck like he was one of her own. I'd visit her a few times a week, and sometimes when I went to her front door I'd see Justin's shoes in the hallway. She had already invited him over. I'd walk inside and see him lying across the couch, watching the Outdoor Channel while my mom cooked him dinner.

Justin wanted to prepare for the uncomfortable transition to his post-playing life. That was a big motivation behind his decision to sign with Oakland. He had spent his entire NFL career rubbing elbows with the fat cats in New York. He was ready to check out what was happening in Silicon Valley. Plus, unlike the Giants, the Raiders offered him a really good contract. I introduced Tuck to business folks around the Bay Area. He partnered with a hedge fund billionaire to create a program that brought thousands of kids in California, New York, Houston, and Florida into a yoga-based health and wellness program through their schools.

It was not easy for an athlete of Tuck's caliber to sense that the body that had carried him so far was nearing the end of its shelf life. I told him that I believed that we control our destinies. Our bodies react to where our head space is. If your head is not right, your body reacts with pains and strains and other physical issues.

The strain Tuck was facing centered on his subconscious belief that his entire identity was wrapped around football. Or at least, his *relevance* was wrapped around football. People had always been interested in meeting him and working with him because he was this great football player. He had the capacity to do other things, but would he really be able to do that once that part of his life was over?

I could relate to what Tuck was going through, because on many levels I was experiencing my own discomfort. I realized that I, too, had to make a decision about how—and with whom—I was spending my time. I believed I was hanging around a lot of people who didn't truly appreciate me. I talked about this with Tuck, and we dove into the things that lead us to seek value from people to whom we have no attachment. My grandma would call me, but I only had like ten minutes to talk, when I should have been giving her the world. There's no one who loves and appreciates me more than her. Why was I in such a rush to hang up?

Part of it was that I knew her love was already in the bank. It wasn't going anywhere. So instinctively I wanted to go out into the world and seek more of it. That set me on a path to emotional bankruptcy. Because of the success I was having at Empower and in the NFL, I was getting invited to a lot of dinners, events, and galas. It was exciting at first. *Look who I'm hanging out with! I made it!* I believed, not altogether incorrectly, that by mingling in these circles I would have access to great ideas as well as some business capital.

But collecting people has never been my thing. I'm diplomatic about my relationships, but I'm very selective about who gets close. It's like that famous quote from Al Capone: "Be careful who you call your friends. I'd rather have four quarters than one hundred pennies." My pockets were overflowing with pennies, and it was weighing me down. This was all happening not long after I lost my father. It was a very disorienting time.

One day, Tuck and I were talking about all of this as we walked down a street in San Francisco. We were hungry, so we ducked inside a Chipotle to continue the conversation. The place was mostly empty and we sat in a booth in the back. We talked about all the things he wanted to do with his philanthropy after he was through playing, how he could use this incredible platform he had to serve others. We also talked about how I needed to stop chasing acceptance. Instead of going to some soulless dinner, I should spend that time with my grandma, my mom, my siblings, my sister-in-law, and other close loved ones. Those are people who love the real version of me.

There we were, two meatheads eating burritos at Chipotle, getting all teary-eyed as we bared our souls. I learned that day that while it might be uncomfortable to unload a pocket full of pennies, it's worth the effort knowing that in the end you will carry something far more valuable.

———

After his first season in Oakland, the Raiders offered Justin a contract extension, but he knew it was time to wind things down. He had put together an amazing career and wanted to enjoy the rest of his life without too many injuries. His goal was to play one more season and finish out his career on a positive note.

Unfortunately, in October 2015, Tuck tore a pectoral muscle five games into the season. That ended his career. When the season was over, he and his wife, Lauran, moved back to the East Coast with their two boys, Jayce and Jonah, whom I call my nephews. Justin settled into a comfortable, retired life. He played lots of golf and spent the kind of time with his family he never could spend while he played. When the kids got a little older, he indulged them in a common family ritual around the dinner table called "my favorite part of the day." Night after night, when it came to Justin's turn, he didn't have much to say. It dawned on him that his kids would never have any memories of him as an NFL player. What would they know of their father? That he was a lazy guy who lounged around, watched TV, and played a lot of golf? How would he teach them about the importance of pushing through discomfort if he allowed himself to settle into a such a lifestyle?

Financially, Justin was set for life, but he realized he needed discomfort again. He thought about all he had experienced, all he had learned, and how he could use those tools to serve others. His mind scrolled through the many NFL teammates who had made a ton of dough, only to have major financial struggles later on because they were irresponsible or, worse, betrayed by slimy, incompetent financial advisors. It clicked for him one night when he was watching *Monday Night Football* and saw an item come across the news ticker about yet another NFL player who was suing his financial advisor.

That helped him make up his mind. Justin's wife, Lauran, had gotten her master's degree in social work at Penn, so Justin decided to follow a similar path and pursue his master's at Penn's prestigious Wharton School of Business. For two years, Tuck commuted back and forth between Philadelphia and his house in New Jersey so he could make his kids breakfast, watch them play sports, and tuck them into bed. It was inspiring to watch him grind through exams and sleep deprivation so he could advance his purpose while attending to his sacred duties as a husband and father. It was almost as if he was addicted to discomfort. It sure made me less likely to feel sorry for myself when I felt overburdened. Once he got that degree, he was able to tap into the many relationships he had made in the financial sector when he was with the Giants. He was drawn to the area of private wealth, both as a way to better manage his own money but also so he could offer his services to professional athletes who needed someone who understood them.

Today, Tuck works as an executive vice president in the wealth management division of Goldman Sachs. He loves the job because it presents something new every day. Goldman offers 360 degrees of services for its clients, from asset allocation to portfolio management to estate planning to taxes. This keeps him constantly uncomfortable, constantly on edge, constantly seeking out the latest information to give him leverage over the competition. The best part of the job for him is that he's on a team again. He depends on colleagues from all areas of the company to take care of his clients' needs. For the team to work at its best, you can't be worried that someone will take your snaps. Tuck brings that locker room spirit to his office every day. It's the same spirit he learned in Kellyton.

I don't see Tuck as much, now that he lives back east, but we FaceTime at least once a week. If we are in each other's area, we will make seeing each other a top priority. He has impacted my life in so many positive ways. He's the one who first taught me to love the great outdoors. Tuck noticed early on that I was too disconnected from nature. So he took me to an archery store to get me a compound bow. I was super stoked when I held this thing in my hands. I pulled on the bow to test the weight, tilted my head, squinted my eye like I had a target in my sights, let go . . . and snapped the bow right in half. I didn't realize that you're not supposed to dry fire the bow if you don't have an arrow. I was so embarrassed, but Tuck thought it was the funniest thing he ever saw. He turned to the salesman and said, "I guess we'll take that one."

They adjusted the bow so it would fit my size and pull power, and then Tuck took me hunting for black-tail deer. I had done some bird and deer hunting before but nothing like this. Bow hunting requires spending many hours in the wilderness searching for game that might never appear. It wasn't easy at first. I struggled to be okay without all the noise. I struggled with not being able to control everything. I struggled with defining my own peace. Heck, I struggled with being out of cell service. But I pushed through.

Tuck's encouragement led me into an entirely new existence. Thanks to him, every year I go on multiple hunting trips to faraway places, and sometimes I don't see a single animal. But it's the act of getting there that makes me want to go, and the time spent alone and disconnected from technology is invaluable to my mental health. I land on insights I would have never found if I hadn't forced myself into such discomfort.

The act of seeking discomfort goes against every instinct we have as humans. Everything we see and hear on TV and in stores is designed to make us *more* comfortable: food, mattresses, couches, TV shows, beer, toys, and the like. We buy air conditioners that cool us in summer and heating systems that warm us in winter. But when you are away from all that, trudging through challenging terrain in weather that can change on a dime, you are forced to adapt to the discomfort. Mother Nature doesn't care how much money you have or how many Pro Bowls you've played in. You have no choice but to relinquish control, absorb what is happening, and build a relationship with a very uncomfortable thing called *silence*. It's an amazing experience.

Tuck and I have come a long way in our relationship, but the conversations we have now are similar to the ones we had when he started training with me. That doesn't mean we agree on everything. In fact, we disagree a lot. We might have to take a walk away from each other from time to time to let things cool off, but then we huddle up and get right back to work. That's what makes our relationship so great. We're both passionate about what we believe in, but we're good listeners, too.

Justin didn't name either of his sons after himself, just like his father didn't name Justin or his brothers after him. This allows Justin to pass along his family's legacy to his children without letting it become a burden. Tuck's dad used to tell him, "I'm a carpenter, so you don't have to be." No doubt from time to time Tuck and Lauran will put pressure on their sons, which will cause them discomfort. In the end, those boys will know their parents are the ultimate teammates who will teach them to press forward, manage their discomfort, seek their purpose, and conquer the disease of fear.

CHAPTER EIGHT

BELIEF

During the year and a half when I was with my father in Afghanistan, I saw a happiness come over him I had never witnessed before. All my life he was so sick and mentally checked out. Now he was healing before my eyes. We were finally able to build a real relationship based on common understanding, with no distractions.

Unfortunately, just as his mind was finally reaching peace, his body started to break down on him. He returned home to the States in the fall of 2005 to get proper medical care. He eventually had a quadruple bypass surgery on his heart. On top of all that, he was diabetic and his kidneys required dialysis. His doctors put him on medications that helped his physical issues, but he became depressed again.

Once my father stabilized, my mother decided in 2006 to go to Afghanistan herself. As soon as she got there she dove into a huge project developing a school near Tora Bora in the eastern region of the country. I was still living there most of the time myself, which gave us the opportunity to spend some amazing time together, although we were often like two ships passing in the night. We'd have breakfast in our house in Kabul, head out for a long day of work, see each other for dinner and a little night company, and then do it all the next day. Oftentimes she would go to Jalalabad or Kunar Province for a few weeks, trying to squeeze every drop of progress out of her homeland. It was a hectic time, but we were doing rewarding, important work.

I spent more than a year flying back and forth between Afghanistan and the Bay Area, spending a few months in each place, trying to manage an increasingly unmanageable situation. It was made even worse when my father suffered a really bad psychological relapse. The first time he broke down, it was as bad as the day I brought him home all those figs. He spent a month in the hospital and never remembered a single day of it. He was incoherent and hallucinating. It was very hard for me to help him from half a world away. My brother, Yossef, and sister, Dina, were by his side while I was back in Afghanistan with my mom so she wouldn't be alone.

By that time I had spent three and a half years with heavy commitments in Afghanistan, and I was ready to go back to living in America full-time. I had grown frustrated with the way Afghanistan operates—or, rather, doesn't operate. If you're trying to create positive change there, you're running in quicksand all the time. Anything good that was happening got pushed out by people who were out to make a quick buck or couldn't stand seeing others succeed. I had proved my point that there was a genuine appetite inside that country for peace and growth, but I eventually came to realize that if I wanted to disrupt on a larger scale—a global scale—then I wouldn't be able to do it there. My mother understood why I wanted to go back to living in America, but she was clear in her intent to finish her work.

My mom would go home to visit my dad for a few weeks at a time, but mostly she dedicated her life to rebuilding her home country. It pained my dad for them to be so far apart, but we all recognized that my mom had made incredible sacrifices over the years so that my brother, my sister, and I have the lives we wanted. Now it was her turn to pursue her own truth and fulfill her own purpose.

I had seen with my own eyes how sports and competition could be used to heal conflicts and build communities. I wanted to use that knowledge to make the world a better place. So it was that in 2008 I was ready to start the next chapter in my life. It had been quite an interesting few years. I had put myself through intense discomfort, been humbled when faced with my limitations, built a community, given myself permission to conjure the full depths of my imagination, had a real impact on others, kept my motives selfless, and ultimately come closer to discovering my truth. It was a genuinely transforming experience.

As I reflected on all I had learned and done, all the mistakes I had made, all the frustrations I felt, and all the beauty I saw inside so many people there, I realized that the whole experience was one big testament to the power of belief. It wasn't just the belief I was able to instill in others but the belief I was able to nurture inside my own soul. Belief in myself, belief in my core philosophies, belief in the knowledge I had acquired, belief in the power of sports to disrupt and heal. It was scary, sure, but I had faced all of that without succumbing to the disease of fear. Once you have that kind of belief, you start thinking that you have the ability to create disruption anywhere you go. The feeling was both intoxicating and intimidating at the same time.

If I was going to realize my truth, I would have to continue following that path. I wasn't sure what that would entail, but my faith empowered me to be comfortable with the uncertainty. I didn't know where I was heading, but I knew where I wanted to start. During the time I was in Afghanistan, my American hometown, San Francisco, had continued to grow into a booming incubator of technology, innovation, and entrepreneurship. It was the perfect time to introduce the city to my idea of disruption.

———

I didn't have much of a business plan, but I was bursting with energy and ideas. I had built a strong brand among a community of athletes and high achievers, thanks mostly to Jake Shields's belief that he could trust me with his career.

Jake was eager to have me back. We were making money off his fights as well as his sponsorships and endorsements. He had moved into an apartment in the downtown neighborhood of Soma. I found a unit in a high-rise next door. The building where I lived had a fitness facility, with a big space for dancing, yoga classes, and basketball courts. We trained in that space along with some other people who wanted to do sessions. I would go to events and parties and get some more clients. Slowly but surely, my community grew.

One guy who found me was Danny Molina, an equipment manager with the Oakland Raiders. He was a big MMA fan and he wanted to learn about fighting. He enjoyed our sessions so much that he mentioned me to Charlie Fry, who had just joined the team in 2009 as a quarterback. Charlie came to see me, and we spoke for a while and worked out. He saw the way my techniques could provide the mobility and functional movement required for an NFL quarterback. We built trust over several weeks, and he mentioned me to a fellow quarterback, Bruce Gradkowski. They were competing for the starting position with JaMarcus Russell but, like Justin Tuck and Dave Tollefson, they could compete and still be close friends. I worked with them in a space on the ground floor of my building. I loved training those guys and found it very easy to blend martial arts with football mechanics. As much as I loved MMA, football was in my blood.

Charlie and Bruce were focused on the physical aspects of our work, but I made them understand how important the psychological and emotional components were as well. One thing I learned in training elite fighters like Jake and Josh and the rest of our stable is that there has to be a much bigger purpose to what you are doing or you won't be able to optimize your capacity. I felt it was my job to help Charlie and Bruce understand that and formulate their own belief.

I did all this even though I wasn't a quote, unquote, certified personal trainer. There are a lot of really good trainers out there, but I've also seen quite a few who are causing a demise in people's health. A lof of people make the mistake of thinking that all workouts should result in exhaustion. That's pointless unless it's part of an evolutionary plan. When I hear a trainer brag that he or she worked someone out to the point where they were puking or could barely walk. I'm like, great, you just ruined them for two weeks.

Right about that time Jake was looking for a new workout location. We had a mutual friend and teammate, Gilbert Melendez, who was opening a place out in the Bayview District of San Francisco. I figured that would be a good place to build our client base. After a few more months out there, I decided that I wanted to scale my philosophy, which meant doing something truly disruptive: open my own facility. When I told a few clients this idea, they eagerly offered to help make this a reality.

I found a space in downtown San Francisco and partnered with my teammates Josh McDonald and Jason Avilio. We had limited funds to hire contractors, but with help from some friends in the martial arts community I got lots of help fixing the place up. We knew some guys who could build and paint. Since it used to be a cycling gym, the basic infrastructure was already in place but there was a lot of cosmetic work to do. We built a ring, but it didn't have ropes at first.

From a marketing perspective, I probably should have put myself in the name of the gym, but I felt that would send the wrong message. I didn't want this place to be about me. I wanted to create a community of philosophically aligned warriors. It was the longer, better play. I decided to call it Empower, underscored by our mantra, "Build Yourself."

It took a great deal of belief for me to take this step. We opened our doors in February 2012, and it was quiet for a while. I'd call my mom at night and brag, "Four people came in today!" I didn't have any money for marketing, so I had to rely on word of mouth. Looking back, that was a good thing, because it forced us to build our clientele slowly. The people who heard about us really wanted to be there.

Josh and I each led half a day. We tried to get as creative as we could. Everything was so new and fresh, the possibilities limitless. What kind of experiences did we want to produce for the clients? What demographic should we go after? We decided early on we shouldn't just focus on professional athletes. We wanted high-performing individuals from all walks of life.

As we built relationships with clients, I hammered away at the importance of establishing a psychological connection as well as a physical one. When we worked with someone new, we wanted to know what was going on in his or her life, good and bad, and how all of that could be brought into our training. That meant having honest conversations. When those happen, you find that almost all of what you learn is the opposite of what you expected. I started calling these conversations "game plans." They enabled us to hold the people we were coaching accountable, because we got emotionally attached to their goals.

This was an offshoot of my days in Afghanistan. I remembered the conversations I had with those kids at the end of practice. They were so open with me. They sensed I was interested and that I wouldn't judge them for the things they said. In Afghanistan, the only businesses were war and fear. I proved there was another way to operate, one that combined the physical with the metaphysical. I believed that my ability to connect emotionally with clients through game plans would differentiate me from my competition.

Being in San Francisco gave us access to the best technology in the world. We did total body composition analyses that yielded dozens of different data points. We learned that if you do intelligent things, intelligent people will show up. That helped us branch even further into the corporate world. We added clients who were high-level, academically oriented executives from Wall Street to Silicon Valley. We started developing corporate relationships that allowed us to export these concepts outside of our facility. We were asked to meet with executives and discuss topics from sales to product development to absenteeism to leadership. I didn't have particular expertise in these areas. My expertise was human performance. I knew if people truly understood their capabilities, they would stop making excuses. Physical activity is such a valuable teacher that way. It shows you in stark terms what you are able to do, as opposed to what's in your way.

I can't say I had a master business plan. I just wanted to be relevant. Working with Jake gave me an entrée into a great new ecosystem of entrepreneurs, corporations, and businessmen. I was gaining so much knowledge so fast, I believed it was my duty to pass it on to the world.

One day I got a call from a man who was one of my first private clients. I hadn't heard from him in a while, and he let me know why. He had just gotten out of rehab. His brother had also struggled with addiction. I started working with both of them. That took my belief to another level. I instantly understood how this connection I was creating between the mental and the physical could be used to help people overcome addictions. It was a major revelation. I thought if I could help these two brothers stay clean for a year, maybe I would be onto something. What I was teaching went beyond training, beyond sports and competition.

Thanks to the advice and friendship of another early client, Chris James, we moved even deeper into the corporate world. I was rebranding myself as a performance expert, not just a trainer. We formed alliances with hedge funds, private equity firms, tech companies, and other businesses who wanted to bring this optimization culture to their companies.

We tested out this model by opening up an Empower space inside Chris's office at Partner Fund Management. We later opened three more spaces in other businesses, and finally did a fifth inside the San Francisco 49ers' practice facility in Santa Clara. My vision had grown to dimensions I never thought possible.

———

When I look back at how all this came about, I can't believe how fortunate I was to start by working with world-class fighters when I was so young and inexperienced. I had not done nearly enough to earn their belief in me, but they gave it to me anyway. Their belief propelled me to do great things in Afghanistan, and all those countless hours I spent in the gym training them, coaching them, encouraging them, and most of all learning from them gave me the baseline knowledge from which I was able to build my career and grow my brand.

And yet, I was struck by how often athletes fail to deliver that same belief to themselves. They'd spend all these hours training and competing, and that was it. When they retired from fighting or were forced out because of injuries, they wanted to stay in the industry. I was confused as to why they were limiting themselves this way. They didn't understand that the same tools that made them elite athletes could make them successful in any area they chose to pursue. They stepped into that ring or onto that field knowing they could get badly hurt, maybe even killed. That should have paralyzed them with fear, yet they conditioned themselves to face that fear and push through it. They conquered the disease. If they applied even a quarter of that belief in another space, they could really go places, because so many other people are reluctant to put their balls on the line when it really counts. It was the same principles, same tools, just a different arena. But they never saw the correlation.

I'd see the same dynamic when wealthy CEOs and leaders of industry would come through Empower. We'd have a tough workout and then I would pull them aside. "I've seen you do three bear crawls now and push yourself through the finish line, even though you could do a lot more," I'd say. "Do you do that in your business? Do you do that with your relationships? Do you do that with tasks that should be really important to you? Sometimes I see you stop when you have the capability to push more. Why didn't you?"

I learned a very important lesson in all of this. Many times people have belief in themselves, but that belief won't propel them toward their truth if it doesn't combine with intentionality. Everybody has these great ideas about wanting to be rich and successful. But if you don't channel those ideas properly, they won't add to your belief.

It's like when people say they believe in God. They pray every day and do all the "right" rituals and practices. But do they truly have a commitment to be at one with God at all times? Do they have the intention to follow through on their beliefs when it's hard? Praying is nice, but we don't serve God just through praying, we serve God by the way we treat our fellow man, by not gossiping or hurting people. Like everything else that matters in life, it's a deliberate, constant practice.

If you meet a man or woman and decide you want to make that person your spouse, what do you do? You show that person the best version of yourself. It's like the standard line from your girlfriend's father, who after dinner one night corners you in the den and asks, "What are your *intentions*?" Those are the responsibilities that come when you try to follow through on your beliefs. It's the difference between starry-eyed dreaming and putting your belief into practice.

We are all afraid of being judged. We can let it defeat us, or we can use it as motivation to push through discomfort. That's where the gains happen. That's how we become empowered. So when we come face-to-face with our fears, we should embrace them, not run from them. That is the essence of belief.

Growing belief inside my soul and then passing it to other people through physical exertion, athletics, and honest conversations became my life's mission. I was not lacking for belief in myself, but, like everyone else, there would be critical junctures when I needed someone to believe in me in order to move me closer to my truth. Sometimes, the belief from just a single person, delivered at the right time, in the right way, with the right words, can make all the difference. Such was the case one day when an NFL head coach walked into my life, literally off the street, and changed everything through the power of his belief.

The Game Plan: Tom Cable's Gift of Belief

It was quite a sight: a wide-shouldered, square-jawed, six-foot-three, three-hundred-pound man with mammoth calves and a shaved head, watching us intently through the street window. I knew exactly who he was: Tom Cable, head coach of the Oakland Raiders. I had been told he was coming but wasn't sure when. I waved him inside and tried to say hello, but he shooed me away and told me to continue working. Tom climbed a few stairs so he could take in the action without being disruptive.

This was in 2009, right before I started Empower. I was working in an unused space inside my apartment building with Charlie Frye, one of the Raiders' backup quarterbacks. Charlie and his fellow backup QB, Bruce Gradkowski, had been telling Coach Cable about our sessions. They told him they thought he and I would be in philosophical alignment, as did Danny Molina, the equipment manager, who was also a close friend.

Tom arrived with a healthy skepticism. He had heard a lot of different trainers doing the rah-rah thing, guys whose main purpose seemed to be to hear themselves talk. He wanted to know if I really was different. He had googled me and learned that I wasn't the biggest guy in the world, but I had gone to Fresno State and turned myself into the first Afghan American linebacker in Division I, and later a fullback, and then gone on to train MMA champions. He figured I was worth checking out.

Charlie and I continued our session. The space looked like a dance floor, which was appropriate for some of the work we were doing. When the workout was over, Tom peppered me with questions. "What about offensive linemen?" he asked. I showed him hand-to-hand and positioning techniques from martial arts that would be extremely relevant for run protection schemes and pass protection. These were designed to use leverage and positioning to create momentum. "What about defensive linemen?" I showed him how to use really violent hand-to-hand techniques to create disruption in the opposition. His eyes got wide. It was as if he were seeing the game of football in a whole new way.

He asked if I wanted to get some dinner. So Charlie, Danny, and I took Tom to our favorite local spot, Pazzia. As we ate, Cabes continued to ask all kinds of questions about my life, so I told him about my family history and my time spent in Afghanistan. I told him how I had convinced the Taliban to support my effort to teach Afghan girls how to box, and how I had come back to America so I could build platforms that spread my perspective on our relationship with truth. Tom listened intently and asked smart questions. At one point he wanted to know what I planned to do with all these experiences. "I want to reconcile peace with humans through the power of sports," I answered matter-of-factly. I could see the confusion etched on his face. How could this twenty-five-year-old kid be talking that way?

When the check came, everyone tried to grab it, but I got there the quickest. Then I looked at the tab and saw it was over $500 because Tom had ordered an expensive bottle of wine. Charlie and Danny cracked up because they knew it was about half of what I had in the bank. "We better double up on our sessions," I said as I paid.

We left the restaurant and walked to our cars. Danny and Charlie hung back so Tom and I could have our space. I walked Tom to his car and we shook hands. "I just want you to know," he said, "that it has been an absolute honor to meet you."

Now, I was already possessed of a lot of belief in myself, but when I heard those words come out of the mouth of an NFL head coach, they hit me like a lightning bolt. Think about it. I was twenty-five years old and just figuring out what I wanted to do with my life. I had been grinding for so long, so often fueled by fear and self-doubt, that I rarely stopped to appreciate what I was building. Then here came this prominent American, this NFL head coach, saying *he* was honored to meet *me*. For the first time in my life, I really felt proud of myself.

It was a tremendous gift Tom gave me that day, and every day since then: the gift of belief. That moment taught me how belief can change the world.

———

Tom isn't a man of many words, but I wouldn't describe him as the strong, silent type. He is expressive and refreshingly precise with his language. He doesn't like to waste anything, especially time.

It's about what you would expect from a guy who grew up on a dairy farm. Tom was born in Merced, California, but when he was two years old his family moved to Snohomish, Washington, thirty miles northeast of Seattle. It was not easy to live on that farm. When Tom was ten years old, his days started with him milking the cows at 4:45 a.m. Where Tom was from, when a boy reached the age of eighteen, he got a job and started taking care of his family, or he went into military service. But because Tom was good at football and had a high school coach who believed in him, he lettered four years at the University of Idaho and became the first person in his family to graduate from college.

Tom's father grew up without his own dad around. He was a pretty gruff guy who let Tom and his sister know he expected them to do their share of the work. Not surprisingly, he wasn't the touchy-feely type. If something was broken, or if something was wrong with the car, they fixed it together. He taught Tom the value of doing things right the first time, because if it wasn't right his dad would make Tom do it again. But if Tom did something right, his dad let him know how proud he was. That's why even though Tom is also demanding of his players, he goes overboard to show his appreciation when they do something well. He wants to make sure they enjoy their own success.

After that initial meeting and dinner, Tom invited me to come visit him at the Raiders' practice facility. This was it, I thought, my chance to live out my dream and play in the NFL. I was still young, in solid shape, and the Raiders were a shitty team. If nothing else, Tom could stick me in on special teams and let me fly down the field and knock some people around.

In the days leading up to my visit, I worked out and ate like a madman. When I walked into Tom's office, I was dressed in sweats and had a gym bag containing my cleats over my shoulder. When he saw me, he laughed and asked what I was doing. "I figured I'd work out with the guys," I said. Tom shook his head and replied, "I've got bigger plans for you."

We walked around the facility and the field. He wanted me to see what a real football organization looked like. I thanked him for the tour, and from there we spoke and got together often, building our friendship.

The following summer, Tom invited me to come to the Raiders' training camp in Napa. When I walked up to the practice field, Tom stopped what he was doing, ran over, and gave me a bro hug. That was his message to everyone else that I was his guy. When practice was over, he invited me to eat with some other coaches, and they talked about how the organization worked.

For the rest of the day, various coaches and people working for the Raiders asked me to sit in on meetings. I watched the various position groups interact. After dinner, Tom told me that they were having a meeting that night in the auditorium. He wanted me to get up and speak in front of the entire team.

I blinked, not sure I had heard him correctly. Speak? To the entire team? What would I say? I was totally unprepared. I thought I was just there to meet with a bunch of different coaches and staff. As usual, Tom injected me with more of his belief. "You're gonna have a lot of guys in there who think their shit don't stink," he said. "You've gotta grab their attention. But you're their age. I want them to hear your story. Just like on fight night, get in there and shake up the room."

It was a lot to ask, but there was no way I was going to say no.

Whatever nerves I had went away when I saw the video the Raiders had put together to introduce me. They had sent a camera crew to our fight training camp and interviewed me, but I didn't realize they were going to produce a video of such quality. It also helped that I had a few of my buddies, including Tom, in the audience giving me strength with their eyes.

I stepped in front of the team and charged ahead, just like I was entering a big competition. I told them my story and spoke from the heart. I talked about training for fights, fighting for change, and getting the shit kicked out of me while doing both. I looked around the room and saw that most of the guys were leaning forward and listening intently. That gave me even more belief. I spoke for over an hour. When I was done, they gave me a standing ovation.

Tom came to the front of the room, beaming like a proud dad. He asked if anyone had questions. A few hands went up, and Tom called on Richard Seymour, a veteran defensive lineman who had just come to the Raiders after winning multiple Super Bowls with the Patriots. Richard stood up and said, "On behalf of the Oakland Raiders, I want to thank you and say what an honor it has been to listen to you." The room applauded again.

"I have a question," Richard continued. "What is the last thing you say to one of your fighters before he climbs into that cage?"

I knew what Richard was getting at, and I had a precise answer. "I say to him, 'Until the death.' Meaning, fight until you die."

I answered a bunch of other questions, and the meeting ended. It wasn't until later that I realized how momentous it was that Seymour was the first to speak. "That dude never says *anything*,"

Charlie told me. Tom added that he had been trying to get Richard to be more vocal because, even though he was really quiet, the guys in that locker room worshipped him. From that point on, Richard and the team would use "Until the death" as their clarion call during pregame, halftime, and all throughout game day. To hear that I inspired this true warrior to find his voice and grow into his role as a leader . . . for me, that was the ultimate expression of belief.

———

From there, my relationship with the Raiders took off. A few more players came to my apartment building to work out, and then once or twice a week I would go out to the practice facility for extra sessions. The martial arts and combat work was the ice-breaker, but it was through game plans that I formed strong relationships. Tom saw all of this happening and made me an unofficial member of the team. When the Raiders played at home, I had access to the players' parking lot, my own locker, and a spot on the sideline as a member of the staff while the game was going on. The level of belief he had in me was just incredible.

At the same time, Tom and I started training at the Raiders' facility. Much like Chris James transitioning his mind-set between his office and his home, Tom came to me to find a different place to put his brain, which would allow him to foster growth and belief. He wasn't just hitting bags and learning to block punches, he was trying to become a better version of himself. We did some game planning and discussed what he was facing as the head coach of this team. The Raiders had sucked for a long time, but now they were starting to win. Yet, he was struggling with owner-ship and others around the organization. There were a lot of egos to manage in that building, and like any NFL head coach Tom was taking a lot of heat in the media. He was never one to think about his brand that way, so he struggled with learning to manage things that were out of his control.

As Tom and I grew closer, I often shared with him my plans for building my business. We had opened the first Empower, and I could see how much potential we had for real growth and im-pact. I had blown through what little savings I had and was in the midst of trying to find some more capital to get over the next hurdle.

One morning Tom sat with me in my office at Empower as I broke everything down. "How much are you looking for?" he asked. I said I wasn't sure, probably a couple hundred thousand. "Fine. Give me your account information." I was confused, so he repeated, "Give me your account information." I did what he asked, and within twenty-four hours he had wired $200,000 into my bank account.

"Take this money however you want," he said. "It can be a loan, an investment, or a donation. It's up to you. Just go change the world."

That's what you call belief.

Of course I took it as investment and made him a partner. I've since taken that equity of his and rolled it into all of my other businesses. Tom never asked me to do that, but there was no other way I would handle it. If there was a profit to be made moving forward, Tom was going to share in it.

Tom continued to be an invaluable resource on all levels. I wouldn't coach a fight without talking to him the night before as well as two hours beforehand. He had a knack for getting my head straight, asking the right questions, getting me locked in. How was my fighter's mind-set? Was I pushing him too hard? In those moments Tom allowed me to expose my vulnerability. He never told me to think differently. He wanted me to believe in myself as much as he believed in me.

––––––––––

Tom and I had become like family, so it was only natural that I would invite him and his wife, Carol, to meet my parents. My mother treated (and fed) them like royalty. My dad thought it was so cool that I had this big, strong, smart, creative NFL head coach in my corner. Whenever we discussed my life and business he'd ask, "Did you talk to Coach about this? What does he think?" My dad was never threatened by my relationship with Tom. He was so full of love and gratitude that I was chasing my American dream, and he saw the value of Tom's belief in me.

Even though the Raiders were showing improvement under Tom, going from four wins his first season to five in his second and eight in his third, he was feeling pressure from all corners, and in January 2011 he was fired. Two weeks later, Seattle Seahawks coach Pete Carroll hired Tom to be the team's assistant head coach. Tom invited me to come up and meet Pete and the rest of the team. I took him up on the invitation and was blown away by the Seahawks' facility. It was on a whole different level than what the Raiders were doing.

Tom had already told everyone about me, so they were super nice and welcoming. Pete seemed very interested and invited me to a bunch of meetings. We also sat in his office, just the two of us, and talked about our philosophies about physical training, football, and team building. Pete later invited me to walk with him around the practice field.

As the practice was winding down, the punt team was going through some reps while the rest of the team watched from the sidelines. At one point the special teams coach asked me to stand right behind the punter. The long snapper fired the ball, and at the last second the punter jumped out of the way. Apparently, this was some kind of prank they like to pull on visitors, but I saw it coming a mile away. I reached up my hands, caught the ball easily, and tossed it to someone standing next to me. The players busted out in laughter and applause. I could hear Tom's booming voice shouting, "I told you he wouldn't fall for it!"

It seemed like there might be an opportunity for me in Seattle. I was excited about the prospect, but the more I talked to Tom about it, the more he convinced me it wasn't the right move. "I think you're a lot better than working for one organization," he said.

I developed an equally close relationship with Tom's wife, Carol. Tom likes to joke that he looks like Brutus and she looks like a beauty queen, and he's right. Whereas Tom can be gruff and give people a swift kick, Carol is more maternal and nurturing. They have a lot in common, though, not least of which is an inclination to skip the chitchat and get down to real talk. Carol has a strength about her, just like my mom. She is not afraid to say exactly what she is thinking, when she is thinking it. It is a rare quality.

Carol was a successful entrepreneur in her own right. She founded and ran a hospice company for many years. It takes a special kind of person to work in hospice care, knowing the patients you are caring for will not be around for long. The best you can do is give them as much comfort and peace as you can. That requires an incredible belief in the importance of service and unselfishness. Her selflessness is not limited to humans, incidentally. Carol also has a soft heart for animals, which is why when Tom walks through the door there are several rescue dogs there to greet him.

When my father was dying, I spoke with Carol several times per week, sometimes several times per day. She never made me feel like I was a burden. It made me feel incredibly special, but this was not unusual for her. Many friends and family reach out to Carol when a loved one is dying, and she is always ready to spend hours on the phone or go to their house to help them plan for end-of-life decisions. When Carol tells Tom she is leaving to counsel a family in this sad situation, Tom knows that that family could not be in better hands.

To this day, Carol, my mother, and my sister are very close. After six years with the Seahawks, including the Super Bowl season of 2013, Tom returned to the Raiders as offensive line coach. That put us back in the same city until the team moved to Las Vegas in 2020. All these years later, I still see him as the same curious, intense, imposing man whom I first spotted looking at me from the street. In many ways I am still the young and passionate kid he first met who was full of grand ideas. Tom has a great knack for slowing me down, walking me back, and helping me plan a smarter path. I'll tell him ten things I have going on, and he'll say, "Okay, what are the one or two that are the most important? What are the smaller things you need to accomplish before you get to the big things?"

Tom has seen me achieve, struggle, and make mistakes. I look at him as a special figure of grand value, the big brother I never had. We are grown men who operate in a macho world yet aren't afraid to say we love each other. There are few men in my life who have had this kind of impact on me. Of all the ways I have been so fortunate and blessed, my relationship with Tom is near the very top. He came into my life at a critical moment and honored me with his belief. I will cherish that for all my days.

CHAPTER NINE

ACCEPTANCE

By the time the summer of 2013 rolled around, my father was in and out of the hospital quite a bit. He was fighting as hard as he could, but he was losing the battle.

Still, my job was to coach fighters, so I devoted myself to his cage match. That meant teaming up with my siblings, Yossef and Dina, to care for him, take him to doctor's appointments and hospital visits, and encourage him to live a smarter, healthier life.

One night I picked my dad up from the hospital, and as we drove away, we started discussing ways for him to get healthier. That started with how we could alter his diet to prevent the inflammation that triggered his other health issues. I had recently opened up Empower, and I was learning about how research showed the impact that behavioral and nutritional changes could have. I told him I wanted him to try a plant-based diet, so I took him to Whole Foods and explained the choices he should think about making. As we walked through the aisles, I could see the wheels turning in his head. For the first time, he was realizing there was a different way of going about these things. It was not an easy step to take for a man who had spent his entire life indulging in the pleasures of Afghani food—meat, sauces, spices, the works. This was going to be, as he would later say, "like eating air."

After Whole Foods, we went to Walgreens to pick up his medication. He told me he was feeling a little weak, so I bought him a cane. When we got back into the car, we sat in the parking lot and started talking. I opened up to him not just about my business but about my truth. "You are the reason I started all of this," I said. "It's because of you that I want to help people conquer the disease of fear. I don't want people to feel the way that you felt. I want to push people to embrace discomfort and accept their vulnerabilities and not feel misunderstood because they don't know how to express themselves."

My dad always apologized to his kids for not being able to do more for us. It crushed him to know that we didn't grow up the way he did. But that day as we sat in my car in the parking lot of Walgreens, we talked in depth about what I wanted to do and why, because I wanted him to know he had nothing to feel sorry about. I wanted him to accept himself, because despite all he had gone through, he still managed to create something wonderful. Right then and there, we did a game plan.

For so much of his adult life, my dad could not communicate his feelings. A big part of it was a language barrier. He was never totally confident in his English, so he could never fully articulate his emotions, feelings, thoughts, ideas, and creativity on a deep level. He felt limited when he was talking to doctors and thera-

pists. I talked to him about that and asked him how that limita-
tion made him feel. "How much of your life did you feel like you
were robbed of a sense of belonging to a community?"

I could see my father's demeanor change. It was as if he thought
that, finally, here was someone who understands me. The waterline was being lowered, which enabled me to ask even more questions. "Why do you allow your fears to shut you down? Why, when
you are fearful, do you think it's better to just be quiet and go
somewhere and sleep it off?" I realized he behaved that way because he didn't think he had any alternatives, because back then I
wasn't in his life the way I was now. I told him, "This is where
physical activity is important."

"You're right," he replied. "I never put all that together."

It was a beautiful experience between father and son, especially when we dug further into the notion of faith. "Did you really
ever understand the true connection between you and your Creator?" I asked. "A lot of our people pray and call themselves Muslims, but they're checking boxes. Are they really practicing their
faith? If you're preparing for a marathon, what do you do? You
run. If I'm preparing for a fight, what do I do every day? I fight. So
if you want to have hope and believe in yourself, what do you have
to do every day? Practice belief and faith. What feeds your soul?
What feeds your head? What feeds your conviction? What feeds
your hope?" We kept going and going.

It was during this conversation that the concept of Empower
truly came into focus for me. I didn't realize it, but subconsciously,
this whole thing was about my desire to be accepted by my dad and
to get him to accept himself. What a revelation! I had been doing

game plans for several years, including during my extended stay in Afghanistan, but it wasn't until that day in the Walgreens parking lot that I realized the entire enterprise was fueled by my love for my father and by my desire to normalize mental health. I had immersed myself in all these different areas, but I had never put them all together. I'd go to the gym, or I would go on long hikes, and they would be the only days when I felt worry-free. There was no medication or therapy involved. Through physical activity, I was at last able to find that acceptance and conquer the disease of fear.

I've seen many people come through Empower with the same destructive mind-set I had witnessed in my dad for so long. I believe words have meaning, so I emphasize to them that we're not working on mental health, we're working on mental *strength*. Imagine how much more help people would get for their psychological traumas if they looked at this as a strength and not something to be ashamed of.

From that moment on, I have dedicated my life to the need to promote acceptance and normalize mental health. That required strengthening not just people's muscles but also their minds and hearts. It required honest conversations. They come to my gym wanting to make their arms less flabby or get rid of a double chin or some cellulite. They're willing to spend hours addressing those needs, but they don't put nearly the same amount of time and effort into addressing depression, anxiety, bipolar disorder, ADD, OCD, schizophrenia, or anything of that sort. Why? Because they're ashamed. But when they come into my gym, they know they are stepping into a space of acceptance.

I knew all of this on a subconscious level, but it wasn't until that conversation with my father in the parking lot at Walgreens that it all came together. I had started with a game plan for him, but it ended up happening for me as well. I could see this new-found wisdom wash over him. He leaned back in his seat and smiled. "If your business was around thirty years ago," he said, "I might never have been so sick."

––––––

It saddens me that we are operating in a culture of shame. We are surrounded by people who are eager to judge us—online, at work, in our communities, and at home. We're scared to do things because we don't want to be embarrassed. We are overtaken by the disease of fear. We allow the rest of the world to have their fingers on the triggers of our destiny, because deep down we know people won't accept us.

I've also learned there's no point in trying to be accepted by other people if we can't accept ourselves. People put way too much value in the perspectives of others. They give more power to man than they do to God. This is the opposite of how we should live. If people don't accept you for who you are and what you believe in, why would you care about their judgments? If God accepts you, who else matters?

This is where I use my game plans to trigger reactions in people so they will adopt behaviors that will allow them to experience the acceptance they seek. There have been countless times when I see people drown in their lust for "things," and when they don't get them they stop doing things they love doing because they feel unfulfilled. Usually these conversations happen after a disappointment or setback. Okay, you really wanted that contract and you didn't get it. Well, have you hung out with your friends? Have you gone hunting? Have you worked out? Are those the things that make you happiest? And yet you're not doing them? Interesting. I wonder why not.

When a person feels that he or she is not worthy of acceptance, it can lead them down a very dark path. We have more suicides per capita in this country than in any other on earth, and 85 percent of those suicides are committed by men. Why? Because we Americans don't confront our mental health challenges. We look at them as "demons" that should provoke shame, not medical issues that should be accepted and addressed head-on. We have created a narrative that characterizes mental health issues as signs of weakness, and we have made it unmanly to admit that they exist.

This understanding was really hammered home when I spent that time with American soldiers in Afghanistan and Iraq. The U.S. military culture is built on machismo and bravery. We've convinced our soldiers that admitting you have a mental issue is a sign of weakness, when it is actually the greatest expression of bravery a man can make. I've had the same experience spending time with law enforcement. I get invited to train with various departments around the country. A lot of these cops are working in areas with high crime and low budgets, and they are struggling with the disease of fear. They also suffer from a lack of innovation and resources to solve these problems at the root level. I've seen firsthand how drugs can give both dealers and users a sense of community. When law enforcement agencies don't have a process in place that provides alternatives, then it leads to outcomes that are driven by fear and prevent people from coming together.

From the moment I gave myself permission to open Empower, every day provided me with an opportunity to instill acceptance in my teammates so they would not have to live in this darkness. I was technically the main teacher there, but the people who came through those doors taught me a lot. I learned what worked and what didn't, not just in terms of workouts and game plans but also what my business should be.

When we first opened Empower, I envisioned it would be a place for elite athletes and fighters to train. The problem was that competitors at that level would come for only a few months at a time. The more dependable client base came from the pool of executives who worked in our neighborhood. Of the eighty or so we had during that first year, I taught almost every one of them, whether it was strength and conditioning, kickboxing, lightweight game planning, or anything else. I saw them earning acceptance before my eyes. Not only did I see the appeal our concept could have for nonathletes, but I also recognized the potential of these executives to be major influencers on our behalf.

One day I was working with a client who worked for a big data analytics company right next door who said, "This would be great for my company." I agreed. So he introduced me to two women who led the employee experience arm of the business. We formed a corporate sponsorship that gave us a steady stream of long-term clients.

I was more convinced than ever that we were onto something, that we were proving the efficacy of sports and physical activity in improving workplace performance. It wasn't just about getting those people to optimize their own capacities but also helping them connect better with each other. It was to their benefit to create a business culture of high performance and trust.

It wasn't long before we had a bunch more corporate sponsorships, which allowed me to hire and train more coaches and teachers. In 2014, we opened a space at the offices of a nearby hedge fund that covered a couple thousand square feet, where we built a mini Empower, with some turf, a mass area for grappling, and an area for boxing and kickboxing. There was another area for weight training. We painted the room in our colors and logo. Because the firm was only a block away from our headquarters, we could rotate our coaches through PFM and Empower throughout the day.

Over time, I thought more about this business model and how I might scale it. I was spending way too much time trying to pitch the Empower concept to individuals. I realized I should be spending that time trying to bring the experience to entire companies. We eventually copied our relationship with six other organizations, including the 49ers.

I veered off in another direction in late 2014 when a client at Empower who worked at a highly respected private equity firm asked me if I would be interested in creating an off-site experience for him and his leadership team. He owned a beautiful compound in Napa Valley, and we used it to host a two-day retreat. I worked with one of my top instructors to sketch an outline of how the program would work. We were able to utilize the topography and outdoor climate to create an appreciation for people to understand the value of learning that exist in the silence of the wilderness, which in times can be forbidding and uncomfortable.

The weekend was a resounding success, and it sent my mind spinning in a whole different direction. I had been doing a fair number of speaking engagements to corporations. They were mostly unpaid—I had no idea you could make money just talking to people—but I did them because I thought it would help build my brand. That weekend in Napa Valley got me thinking that instead of speaking in some hotel ballroom, I could bring these people out into the wilderness and teach them the true meaning of discomfort and empowerment. I called these adventures "disruptor camps," and as I continued to do them each summer they proved to hold quite a bit of earning power, both economically and philosophically.

With our client base so big, we were blessed to have constant feedback. I noticed, for example, that every time we had a kick-boxing or boxing class, the room was packed. That showed me that while we had a dedicated group of high-intensity clients, there was a much bigger demographic out there for us to tap into. I studied other businesses like SoulCycle and CorePower Yoga. Taking a class at those places didn't require a major commitment. You could show up, take your class, and go home. That was hard for me to grasp because I was trying to build a more high-intensity concept, but I understood that I needed to expose Empower to a much bigger demographic. So we took a five-hundred-square-foot room that we had used for grappling and transformed it into a community boxing room. We hung a bunch of heavy water bags and designed a thirty-minute fitness class with dark lighting and loud music. The clients loved it.

Chris James has always had a knack for asking me the question that spurs an idea that allows me to scale my beliefs. One

time he asked, "What is the market telling you about your business?" I told him, "People are loving this boxing program we
started." His suggestion then was to build a business out of that. I
was discussing this idea in the office with my CFO one day when
Jed York wandered by. We waved him inside and asked what he
thought. "This sounds awesome," Jed said. "It's exactly the type of
stuff I want to be involved in."

From there, Jed and I formed a partnership that created Form
Boxing. We wanted it to be like SoulCycle for boxing. In late 2018
we opened up a retail space about three blocks from Empower,
setting up the classroom, a check-in area, and locker rooms. Because we had taken our time and planned smartly, we had a steady
stream of customers right off the bat.

Our next step was to bring Form Boxing into workspaces, just
like we had done with Empower. The space inside the 49ers' building was our pilot program. It took about a year to build out the
idea, but by early 2020 we felt confident enough to prepare for a
major capital raise. Then the Covid-19 pandemic hit, and like so
many retail businesses, we were sunk. It was painful, but I had to
bow to reality and dissolve Form Boxing in the fall of 2020.

Needless to say, I did not allow myself to wallow in that disappointment. I knew exactly the next ecosystem I wanted to disrupt:
the U.S. military. I decided that was going to be my new Afghanistan. Much like the oppression of women inside that country, the
state of mental health of U.S. soldiers is something no one has
been able to solve. The men and women who wear those uniforms
are brave, strong, and willing to fight, but they are not willing to
accept their mental health challenges because it's too "girly." If the

young women of Afghanistan needed to fight to prove they could be "manly," the same should be true in reverse for U.S. soldiers who don't want to accept that they are suffering.

My takeaway from all the time I spent on those bases is that these men don't just join the military out of a desire to serve or because of some burning sense of nationalism. It's because they want to feel accepted. They want to belong to something. I also believe a lot of them come to the armed forces already harboring mental health challenges, particularly childhood trauma. Oftentimes, they think joining the military can relieve them of those struggles, when in fact military service, and especially combat, usually makes them worse.

Now that I had some free time on my hands, I could start really thinking about how to execute my vision. I knew where I wanted to go, but I wasn't completely sure how I was going to get there. Fortunately, I didn't have to look very far. As it turned out, the answer had been in front of my face for a long time. I just needed a reason to see it. Once I did, I was able to set out on my next mission—my next disruption—which would take the spirit of that conversation with my father outside Walgreens and spread it around the world.

The Game Plan: Dr. Mohammad Ali Aziz-Sultan Chooses Acceptance

On the night of October 23, 2010, I walked alongside Jake Shields as he marched toward the octagon inside a sold-out Honda Center in Anaheim, California. It was a big night for us. This was Jake's first fight on the UFC promotion after a long and dominant run with Strikeforce and Elite XC. He was facing one of the UFC's greatest welterweights, Martin Kampmann.

Sitting ringside that night was Dr. Ali Sultan, a fellow Afghan refugee and a young neurosurgeon living in Miami. As Jake made his way into the octagon, Ali didn't fix his eyes on the fighters, or even the raucous crowd, but on his Afghan brother, who stood silently, humbly, and powerfully beside this world-class fighter.

I had met Ali a year and a half before in Miami. We were both invited to a gathering that was being hosted by a wealthy financier with Afghan roots who wanted to work his way into the MMA world. This benefactor enjoyed bringing together Afghans of all stripes, and since this was Miami he threw some great parties, as you might imagine. Somehow, amid the superficiality of those gatherings, Ali and I found each other. It was one of those rare, special instances where even though we had just met, it felt like we had known each other forever.

That makes sense considering we had basically been living parallel lives. Ali was born in Kabul in 1972. His parents were doctors, and his grandparents were prominent politicians. He appeared to be on a path to accomplishment and prosperity, until the Soviets invaded in 1979. Ali was six years old when his family piled onto the back of a pickup truck along with three other families so they could be smuggled out of the country. They made it across the border to Pakistan and later claimed political asylum in Germany. Ali has a very distinct memory of being quarantined for a number of days in an airport in Germany. At one point someone brought a platter of food where all the refugees were bunking up, and everybody scrambled to grab as much bread as they could before it ran out. There was a lot of hunger and desperation in that room, but not a lot of empathy. It made a lasting impression.

One day while staying in a hotel in Germany, Ali's parents got a call from the front lobby. An American doctor, John Haswell, who knew them from their time in Moscow, had showed up out of the blue saying he had been looking for them for two years, and he wanted to sponsor them so they could come to America. It was as if an angel had descended from heaven! The man brought them to Vincennes, Indiana, where he provided them with a lovely home with a refrigerator full of A&W root beer. They were basically the only foreigners in town, but they were accepted into a loving community.

By the time Ali got to high school, the family had moved to Virginia. Even though his parents had been prominent doctors back home, they never complained when they worked as a janitor, or in a bakery, or as an orderly in the hospital to make ends meet. Ali dreamed of being a doctor, too, but he was a very unfocused teenager. With his parents away working multiple jobs, Ali ended up skipping school, getting into trouble, and getting bad grades. Despite all that, he managed to get admitted into George Mason University—barely. His first semester did not go well. Ali looked at that report card and realized that if he kept this up, he was never going to be a doctor. He resolved to change his ways and carried that report card in his pocket for motivation.

Thanks largely to his gift for memorization and doing well in admissions exams, Ali was able to get into medical school at George Washington University because of an opportunity handed to him by the dean of admissions, John "Skip" Williams. Skip is a Black American who decided to take a chance on Ali. It was at GW that he decided he didn't just want to be a doctor. He wanted to become a neurosurgeon. Not only that, he wanted to develop a specialty in life-and-death cases like aneurysms and strokes. Out of all the options available to him, Ali chose the hardest lane inside the hardest path.

Why would he do that to himself? So he could feel accepted. Ali was always an outsider who would find it hard to fit in. As a result, he wanted people to look at him with respect and acceptance. If that's all that had motivated him, his career probably would have flamed out, but fortunately he fell in love with neurosurgery and reset his intentions. He fell in love with the deep connections you can make in a time of need with patients; it reminded him of where he had once been. He remembered all of the people who had helped him and the important role they played in his life.

That blend of defiance and desire for acceptance would inform Ali's every step. When he started getting published, he decided to use his full birth name, Mohammad Ali Aziz-Sultan. He did this because of 9/11. At a time when Muslims were being looked at with greater suspicion in the wake of that horrific tragedy, he wanted his name to sound *more* Muslim because he yearned to make an important point that there were a lot of Muslims in America who were doing great things. He wanted the public to accept him for who he really was.

When I first met Ali in late 2008, I was transitioning out of Afghanistan. His marriage to his college girlfriend had recently ended, and he was working more than one hundred hours a week.

He was full of stress and emotional pain and was not at all accepting of himself. Since he was in South Beach and financially sound, it wasn't hard to fill that void. He got himself a dope-ass car, and a killer apartment overlooking the ocean and dove into the social scene. Not surprisingly, that did not bring him much fulfillment.

Ali had studied some martial arts growing up, so he became a big MMA fan. That was another similarity between us, but our connection was more primal. From that very first conversation, we both sensed that we operated on a different wavelength than most people. There was a level of depth, combined with integrity, that drew us in. Talking to Ali was like talking to a brother, and I know he felt the same way. When I told him about my years in Afghanistan and the disruption I was trying to create there, his eyes melted. "That's exactly what I'm hoping to do," he said, "except through medicine."

Ali seemed surprised that we hadn't met before, but I told him that I didn't associate with a lot of Afghans in the United States because of the resentment I felt from the community where I grew up. I was doing a lot of cool shit, but it felt like none of those guys were cheering for me. It was my white American friend Dave Tollefson who cried when he saw me running up the ramp as a member of the Fresno State football team. None of my Afghan so-called friends cared to that degree. I didn't blame them—they only knew what they knew—but I never felt the support from them like I got from Dave.

I sensed something very different about Ali, however. He was impressed with what I was doing, and he wanted to share in that experience with me. Two days before that big fight in Anaheim,

Ali called me out of the blue and said he had come to town just so he could see me in action. He was staying in Hollywood, and I was so touched, I made the long drive from Anaheim two days before the fight so I could meet him for dinner.

Ali had no way of profiting from what I was doing. He just got a kick out of seeing a fellow Afghan live out his truth. His attitude made me love the whole Afghan community in a new and deeper way. Knowing that someone like him was accepting me with his whole heart gave me an even greater sense of purpose. It made me want to keep fighting.

––––––

I returned to Miami a few more times for those gatherings, and I always made a point to spend time with Ali. In the years that followed, we stayed in touch and talked a bunch on the phone. He describes himself as nerdy, but he is actually six-foot-four, dresses fashionably, and is built like a tight end. He seems civilized, but he's still got a lot of dog in him from how he grew up. I love that about him.

When Ali was still in med school, he did a rotation in hospice. One patient was the uncle of a guy that Ali knew from college. He and the guy never got along, but when the guy's uncle died, he and Ali shared an emotional hug. It was an important reminder that when people are hurting, they are able to let in the light of hope and the blessing of acceptance.

As I watched Ali's meteoric rise, I tried to give him the same level of support and acceptance he had offered to me. He got married again in 2013, and he and his new wife moved to Boston, where he joined the faculty at Harvard Medical School. He also took a position on the staff at the prestigious Brigham and Women's Hospital, where he now serves as the chief of vascular and endovascular neurosurgery. Ali has published more than one hundred peer-reviewed articles and book chapters, each of which carries his very Muslim byline. He has trained dozens of residents and fellows in neurosurgery, and he is in great demand to speak across the country at national and international cerebrovascular conferences.

Medicine has proved to be a path to acceptance, humility, peace, and happiness for Ali. Every patient he meets is struggling with the most profound diagnosis. Every family he meets is enduring a painful crisis. Oftentimes, he saves the patient's life, but sometimes it goes the other way. Regardless of the outcome, Ali's presence creates a deep bond with that family. Sad as those moments can be, for Ali they can be beyond meaningful because they connect him deeply with his fellow man.

That desire to serve has prompted Ali to go back to Afghanistan for several extended visits. His aunt was the country's minister of health, so he was able to work in hospitals and make close connections with people on the ground. He has also brought aspiring Afghan doctors to the States to train. He serves on the board of directors of the Afghan American Community Organization. When the group holds an event, it attracts more than one thousand attendees from all walks of life.

Ali has been invited to speak at these conferences, and when he does, his message is much different from what people are expecting. Instead of boasting about all the great things he has accomplished—and there are many—he talks about the hardships he's faced and the mistakes he's made. He explains to his young audiences how he was able to persevere because of the culture of grit and service that was instilled in him by his Afghan parents. You can imagine how that resonates with those young students. Instead of feeling intimidated, they feel empowered. They feel accepted. Only the truth can create that type of magic.

———

So this nerdy, misfit son of Afghan refugees went to college, completed medical school, studied to be a neurosurgeon, got a job at a prominent Boston hospital, joined the faculty at Harvard, married a beautiful girl, and had three sons. Pretty incredible, right? Only for him, it *still* wasn't enough. So in the spring of 2019 Ali completed his master's in business administration at the Massachusetts Institute of Technology. He did this because he wanted to learn more about innovation and logistics so he could bring his medical knowledge into the world.

I've never put Ali through a physical training session, but there was one period when we did a game plan. It happened in the spring of 2020. Ali's wife had just given birth to their third child, and their world had been rocked by Covid-19. People don't stop having strokes and aneurysms because there's a pandemic going on, so Ali still had to perform lifesaving surgeries. He was petrified that he might bring the virus home to his young family, as early on in the pandemic there was no understanding of the severity of the disease. He showered repeatedly after surgeries and took all the contact precautions he could, but it was a highly stressful situation, and he felt himself losing control. He had trouble sleeping as the anxiety built. He even checked on his estate plans to make sure his family was taken care of if he died, as he saw colleagues getting sick. He was, in other words, succumbing to the disease of fear.

He called me and told me what he was experiencing. There were a lot of things hitting him that were beyond his control, but he was having a hard time accepting that. That kept him from focusing on the things he *could* control, like his physical health, his mental state, his commitment to his craft, and his communication with others. So we did a game plan. I encouraged him to rewind to the beginning of his life and remember his early struggles. There was a time in Ali's life where he experienced so much pain that he almost stopped noticing it, but now those days seemed like a distant memory. Ali was living out his dreams—dream home, dream job, dream brand, dream family. He had a shit-ton of things to lose, and it was scaring him to death. As a result, he was no longer able to take necessary risks and make hard choices.

I reminded him of all of this. Then I reminded him to return to his faith and that our relationship with God can only come through constant practice. This is what allows us to understand that pain is an opportunity. Ali's faith is what got him through all those childhood struggles and propelled him to such success. Along the way he started to believe he was immune to pain. When he felt it again, it was debilitating because he was out of practice with his faith.

Over the course of several conversations, we brought his mind back into balance. Ali was able return to that operating room, dive with his instruments into another human being's brain, and get lost in the process. It's the same bliss that overtakes Marshawn Lynch when he runs with a football or Jake Shields when he steps inside an octagon. When a genius gets into the details of performing his craft, his mind goes into a flow state that is immensely peaceful. That's what acceptance feels like.

———

As upsetting as it was for me to shut down Form Boxing in the spring of 2020, it also freed me up to devote more time and energy to my next major disruption. I was trying to figure out how I would execute my vision when Ali told me about an exciting new initiative he was developing at Harvard.

The endeavor stemmed from an assignment Ali had given while he was pursuing his MBA at MIT. It centered on digital phenotyping, which is a sophisticated way of measuring all the little ways in which people interact with digital devices, especially their smartphones. Think about it. We are closer to our phones than to any human, including our spouses. Ali's objective was to use that relationship to measure all sorts of behavioral patterns, from sleeping to physical activity to communications, that would help doctors diagnose and treat mental illnesses. This was based on the work of Dr. JP Onnela, who identified more than forty metrics that can be plugged into an algorithm and predict outcomes in patients with a high degree of success.

For example, when people are slipping into depression, they tend to stay at home more. That can be detected through GPS technology. The same goes for symptoms of ALS, concussions, depression, anxiety, PTSD, schizophrenia, and lots of other mental disorders. When someone is trying to overcome an addiction, he might visit a counselor, do a stint in rehab, and go to some Alcoholics Anonymous meetings, but what about all the gray areas in between? A football player might be examined for a concussion and then come back to the doctor three weeks later and report he feels great. But how have the last three weeks been when the doctor wasn't around? The answers can be found through digital phenotyping. All this sensitive information can be transmitted without violating privacy laws, as is always the case between doctors and patients.

In an effort to develop this initiative, Ali created a formal partnership in early 2020 with two of his Harvard colleagues. Their goal was to create a digital platform that would bring these formulas to a wide pool of people. The more he told me about it, the more we realized this was a big opportunity for their technology and my philosophy to unite. I believed phenotyping could be a massive value add to the NFL and its work to help players recover from concussions and deal with lingering medical issues after they retire. So I connected Ali with the 49ers so they could develop a working relationship.

Ali and his colleagues are brilliant scientists, but like a lot of really intelligent people their strength lies in their specialization. Moving into the worlds of business and technology is not a natural transition. Fortunately, I have been able to circulate among a wide variety of experts and influencers. It is maybe the biggest asset I can bring to any cause. I am extremely close with many high achievers from all walks of life, from sports to education to business to capital markets to technology to politics, and everything in between. Ali's group had all these great ideas but not much conception of how to scale and apply them to a wide variety of disciplines. That's where I came in.

For the longest time, I have developed my insights into mental health and athletic performance through my own life experiences. I grew up surrounded by a lot of mentally disturbed people, and I have spent most of my working life game-planning with great athletes and other high-powered individuals. Now that I have three Harvard scientists on my God Squad, I can flesh out those insights in a legitimate, respected clinical study. The veteran population is a great target because you have a lot of people with tremendous stress factors for an extended period of time. Once that study is completed, we are going to bring this platform, which we are calling Form X, to the greatest global sporting audience of them all—the 2028 Summer Olympics in Los Angeles. My goal is to have that become the first Olympics in history to have mental health as its central theme. We are going to use that stage, those athletes, and the power of sports to normalize the global conversation around mental health. Seeking help for emotional struggle should be like dropping to the ground and doing twenty push-ups. No big deal. That's the new narrative we want to create. It is much needed and long overdue.

One thing Ali and I have reinforced with each other is that you can't hold back a couple of Afghans when they set their sights on a grand design. This is in our blood. The greatest empires on earth have tried to subdue our country, and yet they all failed because Afghans will never quit when it comes to standing up for their dignity. No matter what happens to them, they keep fighting, keep pushing, keep disrupting. Just as I walked behind Jake Shields and tried to give him all the knowledge, confidence, humility, and acceptance I could, I want to do the same for Ali and his Harvard colleagues, for veterans of war, for professional and Olympic athletes, for Afghanistan, and for the world. Ali and I have both seen a lot of shit and gone through a lot of shit, both in our homes and in our home country. Now we are living a life of incredible privilege. If we don't reach up and try to grab the moon, who will? If we don't create grand-scale, global disruption, who will?

Through all those years spent talking, connecting, and cheering each other on, Ali and I never discussed working closely on a project like this. There was a sense that at some point our parallel lives would converge; we just didn't know how or when. Now that moment has come. The acceptance we found in each other has empowered us to find acceptance inside ourselves. Together, we are going to export that acceptance around the world, so that people will love each other, care for each other, learn from each other, be vulnerable with each other, trust each other, believe in each other, and triumph over the disease of fear.

CHAPTER TEN

LOVE

All too often, people who experience childhood trauma develop major mental issues later on, from PTSD to depression to addiction, and, sadly, resort to suicide. In my case, it turned me into an intense workaholic. It actually fueled my success and even my happiness. What makes me different from so many others who are pushed by trauma into a more tragic fate?

I was loved.

My trauma stemmed from circumstance, not abuse. I was embarrassed that we were so poor, but I was still able to play on teams and be celebrated for the things I was accomplishing. I felt my parents' love every moment. I understood they had experienced their own trauma and never blamed them for that.

My parents never put their sickness on anyone else. They fought a lot, but so did a lot of my friends' parents. Nor did I ever see them hold hands or snuggle or tell each other "I love you." That was not the way for that generation of Afghans. And yet, I never doubted they loved each other, or their children. They just didn't have time for sweetness. They were in survival mode. Their whole existence was sacrifice.

After spending all that time with my father in Afghanistan, I came to understand that he was never really educated on true love. His father passed away when he was young, and his mother was very protective. He wasn't allowed to run up mountains and jump in the river with his friends, because his mom was worried about him getting hurt. So that's how he came to view love. It was about protection, not compassion. It wasn't about expression and cuddling. That's why he couldn't give those things to my mom.

My father was also raised with the mind-set that you should be careful whom you trust. He was my grandfather's only son, and everyone knew he had come into a great inheritance. He was taught to be wary of anyone who wanted to be associated with him because the person probably wanted something in return. Can you imagine anything sadder?

The first time he really understood what love was all about was when he saw his children being born. But he didn't communicate this love to my mom because he was afraid of rejection.

My mom, on the other hand, was raised by a father who was a legendary military pilot and decorated general but who enjoyed nothing more than playing cards at home with his children and tucking them into bed. She had three younger brothers, so she remained the apple of her father's eye. He would take her to official functions and teach her how to be strong, independent, and educated. He made her feel empowered and protected. So when she married my dad, it was hard for her to come to grips with the idea that he could not love her the same way. When they came to America and he became mentally ill, it was like she had another child.

So my parents loved me in different ways, but the power I got from that love was the same. This was an incredible life lesson for me. At the end of the day, this is what my business is all about. Why am I so dedicated to helping people who are hurting? Because I've seen the power of love.

Everybody wants love, but too many people define it narrowly. If someone isn't loving them in exactly the way they want or need, then they don't think of it as love. And they don't want to love someone else unless that person is behaving and reciprocating a certain way. This leads to a lot of tension in relationships. I believe we need to accept and love people for who they are, and accept their love however they wish to give it.

———

In the summer of 2019, I had a dream about my father. It was one of those really vivid dreams you have right before you wake up, so you really remember it. In the dream I heard him say to me, "Let it go, son. Forgive."

I thought for a few days until deciding what those words meant: he wanted me to make things right with my aunt, his sister. I was very close to her when I was young, but she was at the center of the chaos and pain that plagued my family. I decided to follow my father's wish, not just in honor of his memory, but for me as well. I was carrying too much anger, and it was weighing heavily on my heart and negatively affecting my relationships.

For many years after my father died, I suffered from a deep

depression that no one knew about. I never did anything about it because I was scared of being diagnosed like he was. I saw what mental illness did to my father, and I was afraid the same would happen to me. I was succumbing to the disease of fear.

I tried to game-plan myself and thought about why I was having such a hard time processing my father's death. He always told me that my birth kept him alive, and as I grew older I was more his protector than his son. So when he died, I felt a pain similar to a parent losing a child. I was the one responsible for his life, so his death must at some level have been my fault. There would be times—and I'm talking four, five years after his death—when I would be sitting on my couch and burst into tears for no apparent reason.

I came to realize that I felt guilty because my dad died without seeing his family reconciled. He never witnessed his sisters making peace with his wife and his children. Even though when he passed he was surrounded by his family and could smile at death, I believed he did not die in peace. I punished myself for not making sure his sisters were by his bedside.

That dream finally spurred me to do something about the situation. I went on Instagram and sent a message to one of my aunt's sons. We hadn't communicated in about fifteen years. He wrote me back immediately and gave me his phone number. We FaceTimed that evening and agreed to keep in touch.

A few days later, we FaceTimed again. He was sitting in the garage so he could have some privacy, but his mother came to see what was going on. She said, "I hear my nephew's voice!" She ran over to the phone and started crying and kissing the screen. I had been so angry for so long, but when I saw and heard her and witnessed such emotion, my heart just melted. How could I stay angry?

We spoke for a while that night. My aunt was very emotional. She kept saying how much she missed me, how I had my father's loving heart, how she didn't want there to be such distance between us anymore. I was moved by her words and felt glad for the chance to reconnect. Over the next nine months, we spoke every week or two. She doesn't live far from me, but I kept putting off her invitations to go see her because I didn't want my mom to find out what I was doing. (Yes, I'm still afraid of her. Don't judge me, bro.)

Then, in early 2020, one of my uncles passed away after a long illness. He was like a second father to me. He had had a long hospitalization, and I spent a lot of time with him in those final days. Two days after my uncle died, my cousin was found dead on his living room floor. He had had a serious heart condition and was hoping for a transplant. These two deaths devastated my family.

We had the service for my uncle at the same funeral home where we had memorialized my father. You can imagine the range of emotions I felt upon returning to that building. It was tense because of all the divisions in the family. One of my cousins, Walid Majroh, came over and explained that all of the cousins were supposed to stand together during the service, but he was concerned about the bad blood. I told him not to worry because I had reconnected with my cousins over the previous year. He was real surprised, hugged me, and said, "I'm proud of you."

As I was sitting at the service, I looked over my shoulder and saw the room where I had washed my father's body by myself. I was so overcome, I could feel myself shake. I stepped outside to the parking lot so I could release those emotions in private.

When I walked back inside, I saw the cousin I had reached out to. We walked over to my aunt. She grabbed me and kissed my eyes, my nose, my forehead, my cheeks. I pointed to the glass door and said, "I washed your brother's body in that room." We both started hugging and crying again. I didn't want to let her go. I had carried all this guilt for so long, and here we were together for the first time, standing just a few feet from where I had performed that sacred ritual for her brother. It was a full-circle moment if ever there was one.

After the memorial service for my uncle, we drove to the cemetery. When the burial was done, I looked up to see five deer walking past my uncle's grave. I strongly felt my father's presence. I hugged my mom and felt someone come up and place her hand on my mom's back. It was my aunt. I'm thinking, *Oh, man, this is not good*, because I was about to be discovered. My mom turned around and my aunt said, "Can I ask you for a kiss and a hug?" They embraced and wept as my aunt asked for forgiveness.

I offered to walk my aunt to my car. She had gotten older and was quite frail. I told her the family was meeting for dinner and I wanted to drive her there myself. The two of us had some quiet time in the car. On the way to dinner I stopped at my father's grave so we could pay our respects. This was emotional for her because she was not permitted to come to his funeral. That was sad for me because I know how much my dad loved his sister. I never really thought she was the root cause of all the problems, but my mother wasn't having that. My dad and his sister had a lot of secret conversations the last few years of his life.

When we got to the grave, I said the words I never had the chance to say at the time. "Auntie, I want to give you my condolences for the passing of your baby brother." It turns out that my younger brother, Yossef, had the same idea to visit our father's grave, so he walked up, gave our aunt a hug, and also offered his condolences. It was just the three of us there, closing the circle.

Eventually I manned up and told my mom that I had actually reached out to my aunt eight months before. She wasn't angry at all. "You can do whatever you want," she said. My mom, however, wasn't ready to reconcile things to that extent. She still has some lingering anger, and of course I understand that. My mother and aunt are civil with each other and at least can be at family functions together, but they are not talking regularly. In the meantime, I still check in on my aunt, and I have a good relationship with my cousins again.

My father was fully content when he died, but he was unable to rest easy. That's why he spoke to me in that dream. I believe because of the progress that was made with his family and his sister, he is resting a lot easier now.

Looking back, I believe that dream exposed how I was living against my belief system. Here I was preaching love and forgiveness to the rest of the world, and yet I was withholding that from someone in my own family, someone who had been so important to my father. I felt like such a hypocrite. In the Empower community we talk about permission, we talk about forgiveness, we talk about trust, we talk about protecting your heart and valuing others. It resonated with other people, but I wasn't doing it for me. It took some time, faith, and a lot of reflection to get there. It never would have happened if I did not have a true understanding of the power of love.

———

I thought I knew what love was until my brother, Yossef, and his wife, Nicole, had a baby girl. Her name is Luciana Leila Azim, and she is a miracle. Millions of babies are born every day around the world, of course, and each one is a miracle. But this particular birth defied astronomical odds and required a divine alignment of planets and stars to happen. Only God could do that.

As the baby in the family, Yossef grew up being showered with love. He's a pleaser, and he was born with the gift of being able to make people laugh. He was a cute, pudgy kid who loved entertaining and dancing for people. Whenever the family came over, Yossef would put on gray pants, a white shirt, suspenders, and bow tie. If it was a really important gathering, he'd wear a tuxedo. For real.

When he was eleven years old, Yossef told my parents he wanted to join the Concord police department as a youth explorer. So they helped him get a role as a policeman's helper, and he never stopped helping. He grew up and graduated from the police academy and joined the police force in the Tenderloin section of San Francisco, which is one of the biggest crack distribution hubs in the entire country. He became the first Afghan American officer in San Francisco and later the first Afghan American police sergeant. I hope someday he will be the first captain and then chief as well. I am so excited to see Yossef continue to explore endless possibilities doing what he does best, and that's serve.

Yossef may be an adult now, but he is still that child in the tuxedo who wants to see people happy. There's nothing he loves more than having people over to his house so he can cook for them, serve them drinks, and make them laugh. One time he came home to see that this elderly married couple who lived next door was locked out of their house. When they mentioned it was the woman's ninetieth birthday, Yossef invited them inside and made a big meal for them. There are a thousand stories like that.

I am also extremely close with our older sister, Dina. As the firstborn, she suffered the most from my parents' emotional issues. She saw a lot of conflict between our mom and dad, and unfortunately she became a primary outlet for them. That was a serious childhood trauma for her, and to this day she still struggles with depression, as do I. She is very involved in all of my businesses. She works her ass off and never goes in the tank.

I'm very grateful that my dad lived long enough to see me succeed in my business. He knew I was making my mark. The same was true for my brother and sister. He died knowing he had created this little army that would always fight for the things he believed in. He was very proud of his kids.

It was only because of the love from these people, as well as my grandma and extended family, that I have been able to achieve anything in life. I have prospered in ways they could never have imagined as they were escaping out of Afghanistan. I was always proud of what I was accomplishing, but I also felt guilty at times for living a lavish lifestyle and feeling that my mom and sister weren't sharing in it.

At one point I was talking to Trent Holsman, one of my best

friends growing up, about how frustrated I was with the culture of San Francisco where I was living. I was looking to relocate and started throwing out some possible places. "Don't forget where you came from," he said. "You're from Concord. At the end of the day, this is your home."

He was right. So, in the summer of 2020, I bought a three-thousand-square-foot house on a one-acre lot in the Lime Ridge neighborhood of Concord. It was kind of a risky investment, considering the pandemic had wiped out so much of my business, but I couldn't turn down the opportunity, especially since the house was right down the street from Yossef's. I asked my mom and my sister to come live there. At first my mom didn't want to do it, but once Luciana was born she saw the upside being close by. I also asked my grandma, but she turned me down flat. She is in her eighties and lives alone, and she values her independence. Plus, she's real hardheaded, so I knew there was no convincing her.

It's hard to express the joy I feel having my mom and sister living with me in that house. It's big enough that we don't get in each other's way. The house has a north and south wing, as well as a communal area. My mom and sister live on one end, and I live in the other. From our vantage point on top of that hill, we can look down at the dozen or so homes where we lived while I was growing up. My mom and I go on walks all the time and laugh about how different things are. We'll point out the spot where my dad was taken out in a straitjacket, or walk down a road where I used to ride my bike with my cousins. I wish this could happen for every refugee in the world—the chance to live in a beautiful house atop a hill overlooking the hometown where you struggled and pulled through. It's the very embodiment of the American Dream.

I've invested a lot of time, money, and energy in other people. I don't regret any of it, but I've also realized that at the end of the day, the only people I really need is my close circle of friends and my family. Nothing and no one means more to me than my grandma, my cousins, my aunts and uncles, my amazing niece, and of course my mom and siblings. Instead of investing in other relationships, I've decided to reinvest in the ones who matter most. I'm so grateful that this insight has come to me when I am still a young man. Many people don't realize this until they are much older, when it's too late to make meaningful changes.

My life is never easy, and I would never want it to be. I am living my truth, working comfortably in discomfort, believing in my abilities, practicing my faith, and empowering my soul. I thank God every day that I don't have to look far for the love I seek. It's right there at home, where it belongs.

The Game Plan: Mina Azim's Love Conquers All

My mom was the man of the house.

I'll never forget the day everyone came over for a barbecue. As the men were cooking on a gas grill, the propane tank suddenly caught fire. I was playing soccer outside with Yossef and the other boys when the dads came running after us and told us to hurry inside. They closed the sliding door to the house because they were afraid the tank was going to explode.

Amid the chaos, my mom calmly grabbed a towel, walked

over to the tank, and smothered the flames. She looked at the men sternly and said, "You should be ashamed of yourselves." They could only shrug.

If either of my siblings or I wanted my father to make a decision in my house, his answer was always "Ask your mom." It was hard to get ahold of her because she was working two or three jobs. Our mom was very strict about letting us go places. On Saturday, while she was out running errands, I'd spend hours scrubbing the house. That way she'd be in a good mood when she came home and I asked if I could go hang with my friends. Years later my mom confessed that one of the reasons she was toughest on me was that she knew how hard I'd work to break free.

Dances? Forget about it. When I got to middle school, I sneaked my way to a dance by putting on my soccer uniform and telling her I had practice. She finally gave me permission to go to a high school homecoming. The dance started at 8:00 p.m., and I was enjoying my first-ever slow dance with a girl named Candie Fabian. At 8:30, my sister showed up and told me that Mom was waiting outside in the car to take me home. I left my date stranded on the dance floor.

I was a rambunctious and rebellious middle child. When I got out of hand, my mom would slap me in the face or whip me with a hanger or an extension cord or whatever she could get her hands on. I got whupped far more than my siblings, but believe me, I deserved it. It got to the point where I would laugh at her when she did it. Make no mistake, though, my mom was very proud of her kids. We were always respectful to other adults. They invited us to parties because they delighted in having us around.

This is what it was like to be raised by a general's daughter and descendant of military royalty. My maternal great-grandfather was General Ehsan Khan. He created the Afghan Air Force in 1919 and later became a confidant of King Amanullah Khan. He died of a heart attack when my grandma was three years old. My grandma grew up to become the wife of General Sahw Wali, the country's first fighter jet pilot.

My mother was a girly girl at the start of her life, but once her three younger brothers came along, she became a tomboy. They lived a very comfortable life in Afghanistan, but her father never spoiled her. If he went to an official function, he took her along. He wanted to expose his only daughter to as much opportunity and empowerment as he could.

It was unusual to treat a young girl that way, not only in Afghanistan but especially within the Pashtun tribe. But the general was an educated man, and he wanted his daughter to be strong and independent. His devotion to his country was unending. He served at the side of the king and traveled with the royal family to represent the military at official functions.

They still tell stories about the spy missions my grandfather flew along the Afghan-Pakistani border. One time it looked like he was going to be captured as he landed, but he maneuvered his way back to his base. When he stepped out of the plane his nose was bleeding because of the sudden change in air pressure. The safer move would have been to allow the Pakistanis to take his plane, but my grandfather said he would rather die. He almost did just that when the 1973 coup d'état happened. The new regime imprisoned him for nine months and then sent him home.

When my mother was eighteen years old, she married my father. The union had been arranged by their parents. They knew each other a little bit, but there was no dating in that culture. When the adults around them suggested they should be together, they agreed. My sister, Dina, was born on May 16, 1978. It seemed like they were headed for a lovely life.

Everything got upended when the Soviets invaded in 1979. My parents and Dina were staying with my grandfather at his winter home in Jalalabad. One night as my grandfather was getting ready to put Dina to bed, the house was suddenly surrounded by men with machine guns. They came inside and accused my grandfather of plotting something, but he walked them through the house and showed them all the rooms to prove that it wasn't true. They asked him to come with them and requested he change out of his pajamas. "Why should I?" he said. "You say I am a criminal. Arrest me as I am."

Before the men took my mother's father, he turned to his family and said, "Promise you'll never come looking for me." He knew he was going to prison, and he didn't want his family to be assaulted as a way to get him to talk. He added, "And promise me you will never turn your back on this country."

He walked out of that house standing straight and proud. It was the last time my mother ever saw her father.

When the fighting got real bad, my parents knew they had to find a way to get out of the country. They witnessed a lot of violence on their way out. My mom saw people she knew, including pastors, lying in the streets with parts of their bodies blown off, gushing blood. Seeing those things, witnessing her father being arrested, being forced to rush out of the country, should have crushed her emotionally. On top of that, she had to emigrate to two countries, Germany and the United States, where she didn't speak the languages, and then raise a young family with little money while her husband was becoming mentally ill. It's amazing she survived at all.

She did so because of one reason: she was the general's daughter. His love gave her the strength to carry on. He taught her to never give up, never stop fighting, and never lose her positive attitude. He taught her that life was not meant to be survived, it was meant to be *lived*. And that's what she did.

————

When my mom first got to Germany, she thought it was only a matter of time until she would go back home. Her friends, however, warned that if she tried to return she would be arrested at the airport. She had some family who had gone to the United States, so she figured that was the best option. By the time they got to America, they had also added me to the family.

A lot of parents might try to protect their young kids from such details, but there was no filter in our house. I heard all these stories beginning when I was four or five years old. We lived in a small, crowded house and moved a bunch of times, so there was no hiding anything. My parents disciplined us—well, at least my mom did—but they never treated us like little kids. I'd go to my friends' houses, and their parents would shoo us out of the room when the adults needed to talk. I always thought that was weird.

Our folks drilled into us that we had descended from royalty. Without being disrespectful to others in our community, my parents let us know that we were not like those families. They taught us to dream big dreams and then work our tails off to fulfill them. Not only were we never to blemish the family name, but we were to understand that we were destined for greatness. Whenever my siblings and I had papers or speeches to give in school, we talked about our legendary grandfather. It was our way of keeping him alive for Mom.

Because my mother was working such long hours, our grandmother had a big hand in raising us. She was also one tough cookie. We might be sitting in front of the TV, watching a sad news story, and she'd turn to me and say, "My dad dropped dead in front of me when I was a little girl. I had to go tell my mom and help her get the funeral ready." I have spent a lot of time around really strong men, world-class athletes, and lethal fighters, but I can't tell you how blessed I feel that I was raised by such strong women. Many people do not realize that respect for women is a huge pillar of Islam. The Quran teaches us to respect and value women, because women bear children. It also conveys a deep respect for Mother Nature, which is partly why I am so fond of the outdoors.

This is why, when I do game plans with my teammates, I try to push them to be strong and believe that they can overcome anything. People bust my chops a lot because I am so relentlessly optimistic, but I get that from my mom and grandma. I know what real pain and suffering looks like, and I've seen firsthand how love can conquer it.

When my father had his mental breakdown, my mother had to call on every ounce of her strength. She thought of her father on that mission in Pakistan, and put on the same uniform. Her life became a mission. She was determined to make sure her kids had a place to sleep and food to eat, but even more so that they would have the same love she had. She was much more outgoing than a lot of our Afghan neighbors, and more welcoming to all kinds of lifestyles and beliefs. She even brought a Christmas tree into our house during the holidays. "Jesus was a prophet," she would say. She wanted us to know that we could honor our faith while still respecting that of others. She believed we could stay true to our Afghan roots but still become Americans.

She was basically a single mom from the age of twenty-five. Not just a single mom, but a mother of four, because my father needed that kind of care. She was more of a nurse to him than a wife. He tried to do things to make her happy, but he just wasn't capable. And yet, she never gave up on him. At one point when he was hospitalized, she had a meeting with people who worked in social services and child protection. They assured her that her husband could become a ward of the state, which would relieve her of the burden and allow her to take better care of her kids. She told them, thanks but no thanks. The general's daughter would not abandon her husband.

She extended this love, protection, and generosity to all our family, friends, and neighbors. She jokes that our house was one big mental hospital. It's where everyone came to iron out their problems. My mom helped them find schools, fill out paperwork, manage their finances, and try to stay sane, all while working three jobs herself, raising three kids, and tending to a mentally ill husband. Can you imagine how draining all of that was?

No wonder she fell ill herself. Her first stroke happened when I was in about the third grade. I'll never forget what she looked like when I went to go see her in the hospital. She had tubes in her mouth and her jaw was still out of alignment. I thought she was paralyzed. I was real young, but I looked at her and swore that when I grew up I would see to it that my mother never had an ounce of pain or frustration again.

She had a second stroke when I was in college. Fortunately she recovered from that one, too. If you saw her today, you'd have no idea she had gone through these health scares. She is healthy, vivacious, and as beautiful as ever.

———

My mom thought my dad would be pleased when his family members came to the States, but it had the opposite effect on him. These were people he believed had betrayed him, and he had felt liberated being so far away. His reaction confused my mom, and it didn't help that my dad had such difficulty expressing himself. When my other aunts and uncles came over, that caused a lot of friction. The tension between my parents could be unbearable.

When I got older, I felt a need to manage this anger between them. My dad was hurt, yet he was unable to make a hard decision that might move things forward. They both went to Afghanistan while I was in college, and when my mom came back for my graduation from Fresno State, I could see that she was very frustrated. She was over there trying to Sammy the Bull everybody into submission, but my dad was totally nonconfrontational. It drove her mad.

Her return to Afghanistan was an overwhelming experience on so many levels. First and foremost, she was absolutely heartbroken to see the destruction that had taken place. She hardly recognized the country where she had grown up. She was equally distraught to discover that there was no record of what had happened to her father. She didn't know where he had died, when he had died, how he had died, or where he was buried. During her search she visited a mass grave and saw the bones of thousands of Afghans who had been massacred.

Everywhere she traveled, my mom heard tributes to her father and grandfather. She once took me to a village that was named after the general. If anything, his legend had grown since his death. She felt his fighting spirit inside her with every step.

She also heard tragic story after tragic story. One night she sat with a woman who told her about how she was having dinner at home with her family when a rocket landed on the house, killing everyone but her. One of her daughter's heads landed in her lap. It was one more reminder of how fortunate my mom was to be able to escape and raise her family in America. It fueled her strength as well as her faith, and gave her an even deeper appreciation for the power of love.

My mom did extraordinary work in Afghanistan. She built the first private education institution for girls in Tora Bora and created an economic empowerment program for women, among other philanthropic ventures. It sucked for my dad because he loved having her around, but he understood she needed to fulfill her promise to the general.

She planned on spending the rest of her life there, but she came home in 2013 when my dad got real sick. A few days before he died, my father asked my mom for forgiveness. It was such a blessing that they were able to have closure with each other before he passed. He died holding her hand.

Losing her husband was painful, but as you can guess, it didn't stop her from living. She has continued to consult with organizations inside Afghanistan. When my mom turned sixty in 2020, she started having some body and joint pains. It was nothing unusual for a woman her age, but she thinks of it as the result of all the years of hardship, sacrifice, and sadness she had to endure.

She is still a young woman, and for the most part she is healthy and content. She has no regrets. She fulfilled her promise to her father and helped rebuild their country. Now she is giving herself permission to live in peace. Her children are grown, and she has a beautiful granddaughter who lives down the street. When she first heard Luciana's voice, her whole life changed. She likes to say she will never spoil that girl, but then she'll buy her all these pretty baby clothes that she knows Luciana will only wear once, or show up at Yossef's door with a bag full of baby food she just happened to pick up at the grocery store.

My mom gets a kick out of my career. She calls me the octopus because I have my tentacles in so many things. She likes that I'm a doer, not a whiner, but she also warns me that I'm too trusting. That's another trait I got from her. My father used to chide her for the same thing and encourage her to keep our troubles to ourselves instead of blabbing them to all her friends and relatives. She would shrug and say, "Why should I do that? I don't have any secrets."

In one sense, my father was right. If you trust too much, you get burned sometimes. That, however, is the price we pay for having an open, loving heart. No man can hurt us when God is alongside. I hope my mother sees a lot of herself, and her father, in me. It's only because of her that I am living out my truth and fulfilling my purpose. I am who I am because the general's daughter chose love over fear.

SMILING AT LIFE

In the spring of 2021, I went to Los Angeles to conduct my annual six-week training camp for NFL clients. I was super psyched to get into great shape with them, but my body had other ideas. My back was absolutely killing me, and it was hindering my every move. I've been struggling with back pain for years, but I could usually get through it with physical therapy, acupuncture, medicine, and sheer will. This time, however, was different. My back didn't just hurt, it got extremely tight. In order to compensate, my body started to shift, which put even more pressure on my spine and my intestines.

Things deteriorated to the point where I could hardly walk. I felt like my spine was going to explode. I was up to more than two dozen ibuprofen pills per day because I had built up so much tolerance. That tore up my insides and did little to relieve my pain. For so much of my life I had convinced myself I could power through these things with mental toughness, but this time my body was not giving way.

I felt like a kid who had been grounded. There I was, living in a rented house on the beach, but I couldn't stroll on the sand or go into the water. I had this kickass private facility where some of the world's greatest athletes were working out, but I couldn't jump in with them. I couldn't stand or sit, so I had to put cushions on the ground so I could lie on them for long stretches. Sometimes I would have to lie down. When the sessions were over, a friend would have to help carry me out.

I was obviously in bad shape, but I refused to get an MRI because I was scared of the truth. I had been through several surgeries dating back to my college days, and they were miserable experiences that didn't help much. Eventually, I couldn't take it anymore. I finally reached out to my good friend and teammate Dr. Ali Sultan. I texted a picture of myself shirtless, because I wanted to know if this was a normal reaction to back pain. He was greatly concerned and connected me with a top surgeon in Southern California named Dr. Kapil Moza, who arranged for me to get an MRI taken of my back. When Dr. Moza saw the image, he called me and was very direct. "You need to get on an operating table immediately," he said. "This cannot wait."

This was unwelcome news, to say the least. Dr. Moza explained that I had a fracture in my spine as well as two discs that had herniated to 8.5 millimeters. There were also fragments of vertebrae floating around my spine, which explained why my spine hurt so much. I also had a couple of bulging discs. If I didn't get this fixed immediately, I was at risk of permanently losing the ability to use my left leg.

I realized I had no choice. I can be a bit dramatic about these things, so even though I knew I was in the hands of one of the world's greatest neurosurgeons, I called my accountant to make sure my affairs were in order just in case things went drastically wrong. Dr. Moza explained to me that this surgery was very risky. There was a real possibility that I was going to be immobile in my left leg or have permanent bladder issues, or both. Still, electing not to have the surgery was not an option, so I agreed to go under the knife—again.

Because of the Covid-19 pandemic, I had to check into the hospital by myself and could not have any visitors. I arrived at the surgical center and went through the process of undressing, climbing into bed, going through all the presurgery protocols. Finally, they wheeled me into the operating room. The anesthesiologist stood over me and explained he would begin to administer the sleep medicine. He told me to slowly count my breaths.

As I took each breath, a wonderful feeling of serenity overcame me, and it wasn't because of the anesthetic. *One . . . two . . . three . . .* I visualized all the victories I had earned over the course of my life. *Four . . . five . . . six . . .* I thought about my family, my friends, my businesses, my relationships. *Seven . . . eight . . . nine . . .* I spoke with God and asked for a quality life, promising I would make the most of that second chance. *Ten . . . eleven . . . twelve . . .*

Finally, I thought of my father, and how he had smiled when he took his last breath. By that point I was feeling almost giddy. I broke out into a big grin. I looked up at the nurse standing over me and reached out my fist to dap her. "Let's do this, baby," I said. Then I was out.

After I woke up, the nurses told me they had never seen a patient going into major surgery smiling like that. What they didn't know was all the struggles I had to go through, particularly in the previous few months, to arrive at that moment. I wasn't just smil- ing at surgery, I was smiling at life. First, however, I had to endure a great deal of discomfort, just like my father had before he could smile at death. The experience was overpowering and called to mind my favorite expression from Bruce Lee: "Pain will leave, once it's done teaching you."

———

As was the case for so many people, the year 2020 was full of a lot of intense challenges for me. The Covid-19 pandemic decimated much of my life's work, especially on the retail side. Empower wasn't just a business for me. It was my personal brand, built from scratch, and it gave me access to a vibrant community of high- intensity strivers. As healing as it was for those people to come into Empower on their way home from work, it was equally em- powering for me to train them and do game plans together. It was my life's work and a primary energy source.

When I had to close down those businesses, most of those people dropped out of my life. It doesn't make them bad people, but it was rather eye-opening, and quite disappointing. I didn't realize how much I needed to be around them to process my feel- ings. Who was left for me to talk to? Who would be there for me to engage with? Who would trade high-fives and thank-yous? Without that community, where would I expose my value?

The loss forced me to do something I have never been com- fortable doing—sit in silence. The longer I sat, the deeper I fell into a rabbit hole of negative thinking. I told myself that an ugly truth had been exposed, that the world really did just see me as this token refugee whom people could use to leverage their own motives. Down and down I went, deeper and deeper into the darkness. I had spent much of my life fighting the idea that I was some kind of victim, and yet that's exactly how I was characterizing myself. I questioned whether I could ever really trust people again.

Does it seem hypocritical that I could fall into this kind of thinking? That I would start succumbing to the disease of fear, even after devoting my life to helping others learn to avoid doing just that? I don't see it that way at all. If it's one thing I hope you've taken from this book, it's that this shit isn't easy. I wrestle with demons every day. Winning those struggles requires daily practice.

It's unrealistic to expect you can go through life without setbacks. That's why we must practice all the time, so when those circumstances come around we are prepared to deal with them. It's like planting a flower and leaving it alone, yet still expecting it to bloom. No, that flower needs water and sunlight and constant care. It's the same way with faith. We must constantly strengthen our faith so when our foundations start to crumble it will hold us up.

Finally, after about a month of sitting and stewing, I got angry with myself. *You are falling victim to thoughts that you are creating. You are paralyzed by fear, and that is of your own choosing. You're always talking about the capability of changing the narrative. Why aren't you giving yourself permission to do that when you need it most? Fuck, man, snap out of it!*

There is beauty in that rabbit hole. Every time you fall in, there is a bigger, stronger lesson to be learned. Eventually, that lesson hit me like a ton of bricks: I don't need to have dependence on anything other than myself. I had put my trust in people and the power of a community, and those can be wonderful things. But I can live just fine without them. I was putting all this pressure on myself, overworking, neglecting my family and my health, grinding my body until my back was literally falling apart, because I thought my life would have no meaning if I didn't attack it like that.

Losing those businesses was uncomfortable, but it gave me the freedom of knowing that I wasn't going to be tied down by a huge lease, demands to meet payroll and workman's comp, and all the other burdens of a brick-and-mortar operation. Looking back, I realized that I had outgrown this part of my business, but because of all that I had put into it I was afraid to let it go. It was a classic case of golden handcuffs. Reaching that realization allowed some light to get into my rabbit hole. It elevated my trust in the process that God had in store for me. I had been teaching this belief system but wasn't practicing it. I wasn't as dependent on all these people as I thought. I could eat and survive and take care of my family in lots of ways.

Yes, I was disappointed in other people, but those feelings existed because I had created expectations about what I needed from them in order to feel soothed. I've had no problem being forgiving because much of it was my fault for setting those expectations unreasonably high in the first place.

I thought about people who had disappointed me. I realized looking back that I had associated with some of them in a very cheap way. I was allowing too many people to hug me, and I was back to laughing at jokes that weren't funny. Maybe I wanted to be tied to their names or wealth. Whatever the reasons, I decided I needed to clean all that up.

God can give us all the tools in the world, but how often do we go deep into the shed to use them? You can't use them if you don't keep going. If the screwdriver doesn't work, try the hammer. If the hammer doesn't work, try the saw. If the saw doesn't work, try the jigsaw. Eventually, you get to the right tools that you need to meet that particular moment.

My tumble down the rabbit hole took me to another level of humility, gratitude, and forgiveness. It was exactly what I needed to shake me up. I despaired at first because of having lost so many things, but those things were God's, not mine. I never owned them, so there was no way I could lose them. The same thing was true with my relationships. Allowing them to end shows that it's okay to outgrow things, it's okay to evolve, it's okay to embark on new journeys and create new relationships and establish new ways of thinking. Once I understood all of that, my relationships got stronger with those who remained close to me.

It turned out that I needed to lose a chunk of my business and my community in order to arrive at this realization. I saw with total clarity how bad breaks serve as great teachers. They make us realize things about ourselves that we wouldn't learn otherwise. These "bad situations" and "bad circumstances" are actually an invitation to a stronger spiritual base and understanding.

It had taken me twelve years to build up Empower, Form Boxing, and my retail businesses. I thought that would be my legacy, but God had other ideas. The longer I thought about what was happening, the more I could see His purpose. But I didn't see it until I had sat a long time in the darkness. Once the pain was done teaching me, I could smile at life again.

———

March 19, 2021, the day I had surgery, became my new birthday. I came out of the operation with a ton of confidence, not just physically but spiritually. I got the welcome news that the procedure had gone well, although I was told I had a long road ahead. On top of the spine and nerve work, the surgeon had also cleared out a lot of scar tissue from my previous operations. That opened up a lot more circulation in that area. Because of Covid, I could not have any visitors, so I stayed in the hospital alone for several days while I recovered. That gave me a lot of time to reflect on everything I had been through over the past year.

Two weeks after I was discharged, I went back to see my surgeon. I was wearing a big brace. He asked me to take it off and move around. He couldn't believe how well I was walking. I smiled and said, "There are greater powers in this world than surgeons." The doctor smiled back and told me to ditch the brace. It would only give me jelly belly anyway.

It is common for patients who have undergone major surgery to fall into a depression, but that didn't happen with me. Everybody thought I was faking it. They kept asking, "Are you okay? Are you sure?" I tell them I'm better than okay because I'm loving this experience. I believe my spiritual breakthroughs have accelerated the healing process. I'm learning so much about myself and enjoying the freedom of being able to draft a narrative and choose what I want to believe. That's the path to peace of mind.

This experience reinforced for me that nothing is more important than inner peace and that it is up to me to make sure that that peace does not get disrupted by circumstances that are out of my control. There is an important distinction to be made between peace and possibility.

I believe this is the lesson God wanted me to learn. It boils down to a single word: *respect*. The notion of respecting myself is something I have struggled with my entire life. Sitting in that rabbit hole showed me that I wasn't respecting the details that made me who I am. I was more concerned with how others viewed me than how I saw myself. On the one hand, that made me successful as an entrepreneur, because I was motivated to prove my worth to the world. But it also led me to neglect the things that were truly important, beginning with my own body.

My entire brand was built on that body. That's what people saw first—my arms, my legs, my chest. I could overpower people, but in return I was neglecting my own health. In doing these things for others, I was destroying my inner self.

God's answer was to take away my physical capacities. As was the case with my businesses, I needed to face the prospect of losing something before I could learn to respect it. Once I accepted this reality, I healed quickly. Think about how this correlates to all areas of our lives.

What's amazing is that ever since my surgery, I've had the most in-depth game plans with my family and inner circle of friends and teammates. Through my suffering and pain, I emerged with an even deeper understanding of their struggles. This time, I will have no problem conceding that my body is not going to be able to perform at the level it has in the past. That will be an adjustment, especially if I ever decide to coach again. A big part of my value in the past was knowing that I could hold my own in a fight. That commanded instant respect. I don't know that I will be involved in coaching MMA fighters anymore, but if I do, I will have to use my knowledge and life experiences more than my physical power.

Solving problems doesn't mean they need to end. It means you've built a relationship with them. In my case, it has meant transitioning into a business model based on consulting and relationships. As a result, I am getting paid for what's inside my brain. That's a great and very new feeling. Even as I was recovering from surgery, lying in bed and remaining immobile for several days, I was able to be on the phone and have meaningful (and profitable) conversations. As I told Chris James when I was in the hospital, "No more brawn. From now on, it's all about my brain."

He replied, "I'm going to hold you to that."

The weird thing for me about writing this book is that I've never been someone who wants attention on me—my craft, yes, but not myself. But pain is a great teacher, and for me to hide that pain would limit my ability to fulfill my family's legacy and help heal the world. No doubt there will come a time when I will fall into another rabbit hole, but I am prepared to face that struggle with humility and faith. I know my destiny is in the hands of God. I trust Him to show the path and provide the light.

ACKNOWLEDGMENTS

This project began in early 2018, when Paul Kix, a writer for ESPN The Magazine, contacted me and asked if I would consent to be interviewed for a profile story. At first I was reluctant to participate, but with the encouragement of some of my closest friends and teammates I consented. It was one of the best decisions I ever made. The publication of that story led to a phone call from Amar Deol at Simon and Schuster, who saw that there might be more to my story and asked if I would be inclined to share it. Amar put me in touch with David Black, who has been an expert agent and devoted friend. David connected me with my writing partner, now my brother, Seth Davis, who created a safe space for me to delve into my past, connect it to my present, and evolve the vision for my future. For years I had avoided therapy, but writing this book provided much the same function. I believe it saved my life, so I am grateful to all my teammates for providing me with that opportunity.

Writing this book forced me to review my own life in painful detail, which in turn made me feel so grateful for all the loving friends, coaches, teammates, and family members who empowered me along the way. I'd like to start by thanking the U.S. government, which took in my family and, through safety net programs like social security and those administered by the Federal Housing Authority, helped us gain a foothold in California as we strived to make our way in this amazing country.

I was blessed as a child to be surrounded by a large group of aunts and uncles who took on the responsibility of being alternative sets of parents for me and my siblings. Thank you to Ehsan and Awesta Wali, Mohammad and Farzana Wali, Abdul T. Wali and Tina Wali, Nahid and Abdul Haq Rahmani, Nasrin and Asad Jamili, Farooq and Salima Hakimi.

I am grateful that so many opportunities in the world of sports were available to me. I competed on more teams than I can count, so I give thanks to all the teammates and coaches who competed alongside me and encouraged me to reach my potential.

My chosen older brother, Tariq Mojadidi J.D., pushed me toward so many opportunities and always pushed to expose me to the stages where he believed I would shine. Trent Holsman, my best friend since childhood, set the standard for how a person should feel when he or she looks in the mirror.

Thank you to all my cousins: Mustafa Jaji, Hashmat Jamili, Salaiman Rahmani, Mostafa Hakimi, Yama Jamili, Haroon Ali, Ali Faizi, Billy Jamili, Hamed Hakimi, Yousef Samy, Roshana Wali, Marguly Jamili, Medina Wali, Mani Kabir, David Wali, Belal Mojadidi, and Bilal Samy. We stayed tight and pushed each other to make good decisions, stay out of trouble, avoid temptation, and never ever take the easy way out.

Thank you to the Empower Gym and Stable of Champions

community and family for investing your time, energy, and grit, which gave our community an identity that is now recognized around the world.

Thank you, Dr. Shah Mahmoud Jaji and Aunt Asia Jaji, for holding me accountable and teaching me that I should speak louder with my actions than my words—to "show the beef," as they liked to call it.

Usama Canon and Sohabe Mojadidi have been incredible teachers on Islamic studies, theology, philosophy, and spirituality. Dr. Bashir Zikria MD of Columbia University, who has been an example of how to become a strong influence in America and the world through language and academia.

When it comes to empowerment, it's hard to match the collective spirit of my teammates at Simon and Schuster. Thanks all around to Jonathan Karp, CEO; Libby McGuire, Publisher, Atria Books; Lindsay Sagnette, Editorial Director; Jade Hui, Editorial Assistant; Joanna Pinsker, Deputy Director of Publicity; Milena Brown, Associate Director of Marketing; Paige Lytle, Managing Editor; Al Madocs, Production Editor; and Dana Sloan, Director of Design. Thayer Lavielle of Wasserman Media Group has always kept me in line, protected my brand, and showed me the path forward that is aligned with my businesses as well as my values.

To my chosen brothers Jed York, Jarod and Vijay Kwity, Marshawn Lynch, Ryan Melchiano, Kais Bouzidi, Jake Shields, Chris James, Bryan Callen, and Dee and Anand Murthy, thank you for always pushing me to capitalize on my abilities, exposing the power of humility and redefining loyalty. I am also blessed to have many beloved mentors who have steered me through crucial periods of my life: Tom Cable, Mike Darr, Mike Ivankovic, Ebad

Mobaligh, Juan Carlos Martinez ("Panda"), and Jason Avilio. To Megan Stoneburner for showing me that self-respect overpowers it all.

This book was improved immeasurably by the participation of several game changers who have allowed me to contribute to their amazing journeys and life missions: Tulsi Gabbard, Justin Tuck, Dion Jordan, and Dr. Ali Aziz Sultan.

Thank you to the country of Afghanistan and supporters like Dr. Fernando Nobre and Prince Nadir Naim, as well as all the young Afghanis who believed in my family's mission to serve them through sports, academics, and capacity development.

I couldn't be any more grateful for the healing expertise of Dr. Peter Goldman and Dr. Albert Salopek, who saved me from great pain and incapacity and allowed me not only walk again, but to run, lift, work out, and compete.

Thanks to my partner in crime, Rebecca Johnson, who wisely reminds me, "There is so much we don't know."

Finally, and most of all, I am so, so grateful for my family: Sayed Fazel Azim, Mina Wali Azim, Dina Azim, Yossef Azim, Nicole Azim, and my sweet precious piece of heaven, Luciana Leila Azim. You gave me life, love, strength, compassion, and constant encouragement. Please don't stop, as I have just woken up.

San Francisco, California
August 2021

ABOUT THE AUTHOR

Tareq Azim is determined to normalize conversations about mental health. This mission drives his success as a seven-time world championship–attending coach in combat sports, former Division I linebacker at Fresno State, Silicon Valley entrepreneur, author, and philanthropist. He lives in San Francisco.